PRAISE
FLY, EJECT, OR DIE

"This engaging book is as riveting to read as it is relevant to apply. It only takes five seconds to change your life . . . and only a few chapters to tell you how! This guide is a must-read for anyone wanting to make the most of agency and choice."

—Wade Whiting, sales manager and youth leader

"I've known Brock Booher for twenty years, and I can tell you he lives the principles in this book. He is one of the clearest thinkers and best decision makers I know, and that is really something considering the company we keep. Arm yourself for the ride of your life by adopting these powerful principles!"

—Marcus North, fighter pilot

"I really enjoyed this book and would highly recommend it to parents, youth leaders, and teenagers alike. The author brings a unique perspective to the hows and whys of decision making . . . from little everyday choices to spiritual life or death judgments. The guidelines outlined in this book are sure to help anyone fly out of a bad situation."

—Jennifer Hancock, youth teacher

"*Fly, Eject, or Die* has a wonderful way of pulling you right into the cockpit! The stories are high adventure and give the reader a good understanding of what it takes physically and mentally to navigate an aircraft. Then the author teaches gospel principles in a brilliant metaphor. We learn about practicing and preparing for life's unexpected challenges. This book is both a thrilling and inspiring ride."

—Heidi Tucker, author of *Finding Hope in the Journey*

"Life is dangerous. Life at 40,000 feet is a lot more dangerous. Learn from an experienced pilot the strategies of pre-decision making and see how it can help you navigate the daily spiritual pitfalls that are all around us."

—Ty Ruddell, Scout leader

FLY, EJECT, OR DIE

FLY, EJECT, OR DIE

UNDERSTANDING **SPLIT-SECOND** SPIRITUAL DECISIONS

BROCK BOOHER

AUTHOR OF RETURN AND CONTINUE WITH HONOR

CFI
An imprint of Cedar Fort, Inc.
Springville, Utah

This is not an official publication of The Church of Jesus Christ of Latter-day Saints. The opinions and views expressed herein belong solely to the author and do not necessarily represent the opinions or views of Cedar Fort, Inc. Permission for the use of sources, graphics, and photos is also solely the responsibility of the author.

ISBN 13: 978-1-4621-2150-2

Published by CFI, an imprint of Cedar Fort, Inc., 2373 W. 700 S., Springville, UT 84663
Distributed by Cedar Fort, Inc., www.cedarfort.com

LIBRARY OF CONGRESS CONTROL NUMBER: 2017955996

Cover design by Katie Payne
Cover design © 2017 by Cedar Fort, Inc.
Edited and typeset by Emily S. Chambers

Printed in the United States of America

10 9 8 7 6 5 4 3 2 1

Printed on acid-free paper

Dedicated to the bold aviators who risked
life and limb to make aviation safer.

OTHER TITLES FROM
BROCK BOOHER

Nonfiction
Return and Continue with Honor

Fiction
Healing Stone
The Charity Chip

CONTENTS

Introduction...1

The Ejection Decision 7

Ejection Training 21

Why Agency?..27

Using Our Agency Effectively.........................41

The Agency Checklist 57

Agency Training..89

What Happens If You Crash? 101

Conclusion...113

Works Cited 117

Acknowledgments 123

About the Author...127

Photograph courtesy of National Archives Catalog
SSGT Bennie J. Davis

INTRODUCTION

In the high-speed world of the fighter pilot, millisec-onds can be the difference between life and death. The photo to the left has not been altered. It is a real pilot ejecting from a real airplane only milliseconds before it impacted the ground. How was it possible for the fighter pilot in the picture to make a life-or-death ejection decision correctly in milliseconds?

He didn't.

Every day we are faced with a variety of decisions. What should I wear? What do I want to eat? What music will I listen to? Who do I want to spend time with? How will I behave today? We may feel as though we don't have a lot of control over our lives, but each of us spends all of our waking hours making choices. Most of those choices are not life-or-death choices, or at least they don't appear to be. But every day we *do* make moral choices that can lead to spiritual life or death.

Moral agency is the most enabling tool we possess. It is a tool that we use instinctively without much training. It is true that we sing hymns about choosing the right, and we even wear jewelry to remind us. However, in reality, we often make the wrong choice. What is wrong with us? Why can't we choose the right when the choice is placed before us?

Since we seem to struggle so much with choosing the right, perhaps we shouldn't be allowed so much freedom to choose. Maybe we aren't prepared to deal with the extensive moral agency granted unto us and would be better off if someone else controlled us. Think about how nice it would be if all of our decisions were made for us. We wouldn't have to worry about making the wrong choice—or the right choice for that matter. Of course, this was Lucifer's proposal, and at the heart of his plan was the lie that we could be exalted by limiting our agency. Lucifer's plan would never work because he seeks to "destroy the agency of man" (Moses 4:3). Heavenly Father's plan is built upon the agency of man, and without moral agency and the freedom to choose, His plan would cease to function.

So here we are. We have been given the ability to choose, and every day we are faced with thousands of choices. We have been given an incredible power, an awesome tool—the magnificent and ennobling virtue of agency. How do we use it correctly? How can we employ our agency when we face a tough moral decision? When a difficult choice is placed before us, how do we make the right decision in milliseconds?

We don't.

The fighter pilot has three choices in any life-threatening situation while flying: fly the aircraft out of the situation, eject from the aircraft, or die in the crash. He can continue to fly the airplane, provided that it will still fly, and eventually land it. He can eject and hope that the ejection seat and parachute work as advertised. He can crash with the airplane and most likely die. Even though it seems like the ejection decision is made in milliseconds, the fighter pilot has trained, prepared, and practiced for hours to make a split-second, life-or-death decision.

Likewise, learning to properly exercise our agency will take preparation. It will take training. It will take practice. Like the fighter pilot, we will be faced with life-or-death spiritual decisions with only milliseconds to make a choice. If we don't prepare ahead of time for that split-second moral decision, we run the risk of a spiritual crash.

The purpose of this book is to help you prepare to use your moral agency effectively in difficult situations by applying the decision-making skills of a fighter pilot to your life.

Disclaimer: Although I use real examples of aircraft accidents and incidents to teach and support specific principles, I do not wish to disparage any of my fellow aviators. It is easy to play "Monday morning quarterback" and second-guess the decisions and actions of pilots after the fact, but any reference to an accident is not intended to point fingers or be critical of performance. We learn from the mistakes of others, and even though I may use aircraft accidents to teach a principle, I do not wish to cast a negative light on the pilots themselves. I only wish to give the reader a tangible example to help understand and retain the concepts presented.

THE EJECTION DECISION

When USAF Captain Christopher Stricklin got up the morning of September 14, 2003, ejecting from an airplane was the furthest thing from his mind. He showered, shaved, and dressed in his airshow flight suit, a deep red pair of flame-retardant coveralls. As Thunderbird #6, he would be flying the show position of Opposing Solo performing coordinated acrobatic maneuvers as a single ship opposite the rest of the aircraft in formation. He had been handpicked from hundreds of candidates, all of them United States Air Force fighter pilots with a specific physical build, a steely-eyed look of competence, and—of course—above-average flying skills.

It was a beautiful fall morning in Mountain Home Air Force Base, Idaho. The sky was royal blue without even a wisp of a cloud. The winds were light and the temperature was pleasant. His aircraft, the F-16 Fighting Falcon painted in Thunderbird colors, sat fueled, polished, and ready to fly. It was a perfect day for an airshow, and Captain Stricklin was about to give the gathering crowd a show they would never forget.

The Thunderbird pilots marched out to show center, and stood at parade rest in front of the six white F-16s with bright red noses and gaping air intakes making them look like hungry beasts. As music played and the announcer's deep voice boomed over the loud speakers, the pilots marched in unison to their airplanes and strapped in.

One by one the turbine blades of the Pratt and Whitney engines began to spin and a deafening whine permeated the flight line. Thunderbird #1 gave the signal and they pushed up the throttles in sequence, engulfing the crowd in the high pitch whine of high performance turbojet engines as they taxied out to the runway for takeoff.

With a nod of his head, the four-ship formation lurched forward together and began rolling down the runway. The formation leapt into the air and climbed away from the ground like four small rocket ships headed for outer space. Thunderbird #5 followed

shortly behind the four-ship formation at maximum power. After lifting off the runway and bringing up the gear, he performed an aileron roll at low altitude, and then turned his nose vertical and climbed straight up until the aircraft was out of sight.

Finally, Captain Stricklin, Thunderbird #6, pushed up the throttle and hurtled down the runway. He raised the landing gear and pulled back on the stick. His craft responded to his input and zoomed upward as the crowd watched. The program called for him to perform a basic maneuver, the split-s—a reversal in the vertical plane instead of the horizontal plane. It isn't a complicated or necessarily dangerous maneuver, but he would be performing it over show center at very low altitude.

He raised the nose and shoved the throttle forward going almost vertical over show center to get enough altitude for the split-s. The runway grew smaller behind him as he climbed like a homesick angel. To perform the maneuver safely, he needed to reach an altitude of three thousand feet above show center before rolling inverted and pulling back over the runway in front of the crowd. The terrain elevation of Mountain Home, Idaho, was approximately three thousand feet above sea level, but most of his training was done in Nevada, where the terrain was two thousand feet above sea level. Because of this conditioning during his practice sessions, Captain Stricklin made a mental error as he began the maneuver. He confused the altitude of the local terrain with the altitude of the terrain in Nevada and began the split-s with only two thousand feet of turning air below him. The mental error robbed him of one thousand feet of precious altitude. As he pointed the nose of the aircraft down toward show center, he wasn't sure what was wrong, but he sensed that he was in trouble. The ground was closer than he anticipated.

He was faced with three possible choices—fly the aircraft out of the situation, eject from the aircraft, or die in the crash. By the time he had rolled the aircraft and began to pull the nose of the inverted aircraft back toward show center, it was aerodynamically impossible for Captain Stricklin to fly out of the situation. He knew that the aircraft wouldn't recover to level flight in the space below him, and he couldn't turn the aircraft any tighter because the laws of aerodynamics wouldn't allow it. He was already max performing the aircraft. He couldn't abort the maneuver because he was past the point of no return with his nose pointing at the runway below. Now he was down to two options— eject, or die in the crash.

His years of training and preparation kicked in. First, he turned the aircraft slightly away from the crowd trying not to sacrifice the aerodynamic lift that would put him into a safe envelope for ejection. No matter what happened, he didn't want anyone else to get hurt. He considered pulling the ejection handles immediately, but took a quick look at his sink rate (the speed at which he was falling from the sky). He was dropping too fast. Even the most advanced ejection seat in the world couldn't overcome the laws of physics and gravity. If he pulled the handles now, he would be ejected from the aircraft but impact the ground before his parachute opened. He had to wait. He continued to pull the stick back to the limit and forced himself to stay with the aircraft as the runway grew larger in his windshield. He checked the crowd; they would be safe.

Anxious to get out of the aircraft alive, he reached for the ejection handle again with his left hand but then checked his sink rate. It was still too high. He wouldn't survive the ejection. He watched the ground fill his windscreen and rush up to meet him, but with discipline of training, he forced himself to wait. He knew his window of opportunity would be very small. He had to arrest the sink rate of the aircraft enough to allow the ejection seat to work properly and hope that he didn't impact the ground before he was in the ejection envelope. If he could reduce the rate at which he was approaching the ground, the rocket motors in the ejection seat could propel him away from the ground (and the crash) to an altitude that would also allow for the parachute to open. It was the only chance he had to save his life. With his aircraft approaching impact with the ground—less than fifty feet—he looked down and saw that he was in the performance envelope of the ejection seat. Eject or die? Eject! He pulled the ejection handle and began the ride of his life.

The ejection sequence started with the ignition of a charge that sent hot gases through tubing to the canopy ejection system. Instantaneously, charges along the canopy rail exploded, forcing the canopy into the wind and ripping it away from the cockpit. As the canopy sailed away, the hot gases also ignited the rocket motors underneath the seat. The rocket engines propelled him—and the seat—up the rails in a cloud of smoke and flames. His body was suddenly fifteen times its normal weight—15 Gs. (The forces acting on his body were so powerful that after the accident, he was an inch and a half shorter and took several months to return to his normal height.) He struggled not to

Photograph courtesy of National Archives Catalog
SSGT Bennie J. Davis

black out as all the blood rushed from his head to his lower extremities. Within milliseconds, the seat and Captain Stricklin were hurtling upward, away from the crashing airplane.

As the seat exited the aircraft, the parachute mortar was triggered, catapulting a small drogue chute out of the seat to extract the main chute out of its casing. And 0.2 seconds after leaving the aircraft, the chute began to deploy. The CKU-5 rocket system ignited, and three small rocket motors continued to propel the seat away from the impending wreckage. The STAPAC (STAbilization PACkage or system of pitot tubes and gyros) adjusted the flow of thrust to stabilize the seat as it hit the wind stream.

At 0.45 seconds after the ejection was initiated, man-seat separation began. A small charge forced the seat belt and shoulder harness connector to release. The pilot was pushed out of the seat by the man-seat-separator motor. The seat frame fell away, leaving him only connected to the parachute assembly and the seat kit (a small case of survival equipment) that deployed via an attached lanyard.

As man-seat separation occurred, the small drogue chute opened and pulled the main chute from its package. The nylon canopy, attached to the four main risers by a series of small nylon ropes, billowed open. At approximately 1.8 seconds after he pulled the handle, Captain Stricklin's chute fully deployed. Milliseconds before, he was hurtling through the air at over one hundred miles per hour, and now the parachute opened and suddenly decelerated his movement to almost zero. His limbs flew forward and items not attached very well (like checklists strapped to his leg) went flying off because of the rapid deceleration. This is appropriately named "opening shock."

Now, after approximately two seconds of violent activity synchronized down to the millisecond, he hung in the parachute harness and floated down to terra firma. He hit the ground next to the mangled up piece of metal that was once his airplane surrounded by fire.

Captain Stricklin had been trained to follow a specific post-ejection checklist. Unfortunately, because of his close proximity to the ground, Captain Stricklin didn't have time for, nor does he remember, any of those post-ejection checklist items. He looked up to check his parachute and realized that he was already standing on the ground. *Well, my parachute didn't open. That's not good. I'm standing up. I'm not supposed to be standing up. I'm supposed to roll. My chute didn't open.*

EJECTION SEAT OPERATION

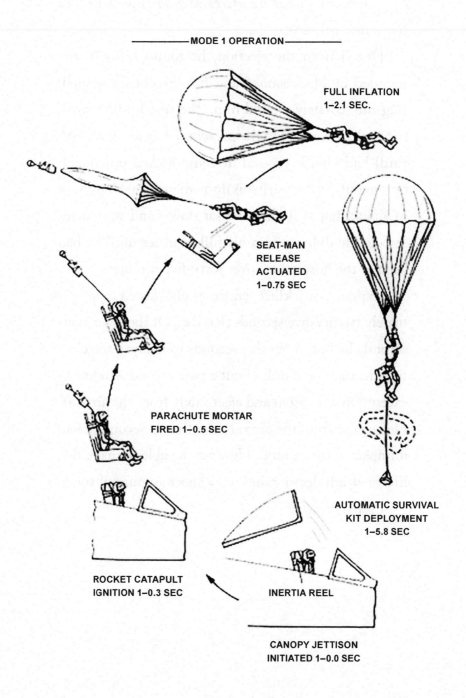

FULL INFLATION
1–2.1 SEC.

SEAT-MAN
RELEASE
ACTUATED
1–0.75 SEC

PARACHUTE MORTAR
FIRED 1–0.5 SEC

AUTOMATIC SURVIVAL
KIT DEPLOYMENT
1–5.8 SEC

ROCKET CATAPULT
IGNITION 1–0.3 SEC

INERTIA REEL

CANOPY JETTISON
INITIATED 1–0.0 SEC

And you don't land standing up. So I guess I didn't make it. This must be what it's like to be dead (Freeman, "22 Seconds," 161–66).

Dazed from the ejection, he found himself surrounded by black smoke and fire, except for a small ring immediately around him. The seat kit (the small survival kit connect to the parachute harness via a lanyard) had hit the ground first and kicked up enough dust to put out the fire in his immediate area. Confused, in shock, but still alive, he sat down and waited for rescue. He didn't regain his full faculties until he had been at the hospital for over forty-five minutes.

Captain Stricklin's entire flight lasted approximately twenty-five seconds that day. Of those precious seconds he had about five seconds to analyze the ejection decision, and only about a two-second window to execute that decision and eject safely from the aircraft. He ejected from the aircraft less than a second before it impacted the ground. How was he able to make this life-or-death decision in such a short amount of time?

Preparation.

Captain Stricklin's ejection from inside the cockpit.
(Gregory Freeman, "22 Seconds," Readers Digest, Feb. 2005.)
To watch the entire video of the ejection, visit brockbooher.com.

EJECTION TRAINING

The human brain can process incredible amounts of information in a very short period of time, especially with the help of adrenaline in stressful situations. But like any good computer, the human brain is only as good as the information it is given. Consider the simple act of catching a ball. It requires hand-eye coordination, timing, almost subconscious motor skill control, and on-the-fly calculations. The first time a child tries to catch a ball, it usually doesn't end successfully. Learning to catch requires coaching and practice. With continued practice and training, a professional baseball player can stand stationary in the outfield waiting for the crack of the bat and catch a fly ball traveling at speeds upward of ninety miles an hour on the run. If we wish to make complicated decisions in a short period of time, we need training, practice, and preparation.

Before Captain Stricklin was faced with his split-second, life-or-death ejection decision, he had given his brain years of training and volumes of information to help with the decision. He didn't make the decision to eject in those few seconds of flight that September day. He made the decision to eject long before he ever strapped into the first aircraft ejection seat in Air Force pilot training.

In preparation for his first flight, he spent hours in the classroom learning about the ejection process and decision. Life support personnel taught him about the proper ejection seat position—heels back, elbows in, back straight, head back—and used an ejection seat trainer to simulate the violent event. He spent time hanging in a parachute harness while he recited the procedural steps to a safe parachute descent—"Canopy, visor, mask, seat kit, four line, steer, prepare, release!" Canopy: Check the parachute canopy for any malfunctions. Visor: If it hasn't already been ripped from the helmet by the wind, lift the visor. Mask: Remove the mask and discard if possible. Seat kit: If the small survival kit attached to the seat has not deployed, release it. Four line: Pull the red handles found on the rear risers of the parachute and pull them to release four lines that provide steering and forward momentum. Steer: Using the four-line release handles, steer into the wind and look for a good landing spot. Prepare: Prepare for landing by putting your body into the landing position. Release: After landing, release from the parachute to keep from being dragged.

He learned about the various parachute malfunctions and how to remedy them before crashing to the ground. "Remember," they told him, "If you have a chute malfunction, you have the rest of your life to fix it." He practiced parachute landings by jumping from a short platform and learning the five points of impact. His classmates pulled him across the ground by the harness to teach him how to release himself from the harness in high winds. He was towed behind a pickup truck in the parachute (like parasailing but over land instead of water) and then released so that he could practice all the post-ejection procedures and experience a landing.

Additionally, he watched presentations about the ejection decision and listened to testimonies of other pilots who had survived ejections and the lessons they learned from the experience. He learned about the mechanics of the seat and how it worked.

Author practicing a parachute landing circa 1989

Next he spent time in a flight simulator with his instructor rehearsing the various emergency procedures and possible scenarios that might lead to his ejection. He learned about dual-engine flameouts, uncontrollable spins, and spatial disorientation. They talked about when to eject if an acrobatic maneuver went awry, if the aircraft caught on fire, or if the aircraft went into an uncontrollable spin.

Together they reviewed performance charts that outlined the capabilities of the ejection seat. They calculated minimum altitudes for ejection in a variety of situations and discussed the various decision points that would trigger an automatic decision to eject. With each possible scenario they did the math together and calculated the performance envelope of the ejection seat, and together they set predetermined limits for the various emergency scenarios. Over and over, he was drilled and tested on the ejection decision, the ejection process, and the ejection procedure. All of this was done before his first flight. All of this preparation was done and the ejection decisions were made *before* he flew his first flight.

Even though Captain Stricklin only had seconds to make a decision that fateful day in Idaho, he had spent years preparing for that decision. He was able to act quickly and save his life because he had decided to eject long before he was faced with the decision to actually pull the ejection handles.

When milliseconds can determine whether you live or die, prior preparation is crucial.

WHY AGENCY?

Nothing ennobles the human spirit and makes humankind more godlike than the power of choice.

Agency didn't begin with the creation of man and the Garden of Eden. We know that we existed as intelligences and spirit children before the creation of the world (D&C 93:29). We were free to act for ourselves, and make choices concerning our behavior, obedience, and progress (D&C 93:30; Moses 4:3). But it was in the Garden of Eden where God first spelled it out for Adam and Eve. He placed before them two opposing options and allowed them the agency to choose for themselves. He told Adam and Eve, "Of every tree of the garden thou mayest freely eat, but of the tree of the knowledge of good and evil, thou shalt not eat of it, nevertheless, thou mayest choose for thyself, for it is given unto thee; but, remember that I forbid it, for in the day thou eatest thereof thou shalt surely die" (Moses 3:16–17).

Moral agency is founded on four conditions: 1) The individual must be free to choose. 2) The individual must have alternatives to choose between. 3) The individual must have knowledge. 4) The individual must be subject to consequences (fixed by law) because of the choice (Daniel H. Ludlow, "Moral Free Agency"; D. Todd Christofferson, "Moral Agency").

Adam and Eve were free to eat of all of the fruit in the Garden of Eden. They were free to choose. The precious gift of agency had been given to them as spirit children of a loving Heavenly Father, and now it continued with them in the Garden. We cannot underestimate the value of this gift. David O. McKay said, "Next to the bestowal of life itself, the right to direct that life is God's greatest gift to man. . . . Freedom of choice is more to be treasured than any possession earth can give. It is inherent in the spirit of man. It is a divine gift to every normal being. . . . Everyone has this most precious of all life's endowments—the gift of free agency—man's inherited and inalienable right"

(*The Improvement Era*, 86). Agency is the freedom to choose.

Adam and Eve had a variety of fruits to choose from, including the Tree of Life and the Tree of Knowledge of Good and Evil. They had alternatives to choose between. Father Lehi taught, "For it must needs be, that there is an opposition in all things" (2 Nephi 2:11). Without alternatives, the power to choose is irrelevant and pointless. It would be like going to a restaurant with only one item on the menu. We would be free to choose but have nothing to choose between, and our agency would remain inert and incapable of producing any faith or obedience. Agency requires alternatives.

Adam and Eve were taught that if they chose to eat from the Tree of Knowledge of Good and Evil they would surely die. They were given knowledge, but only limited knowledge. They only knew of the consequences spelled out to them by Heavenly Father, but they were still in a state of innocence, and "they would have remained in a state of innocence, having no joy, for they knew no misery; doing no good, for they knew no sin" (2 Nephi 2:23). Fortunately for us, they chose to transgress (not sin, because sinning required greater knowledge than they possessed at the time) and partook of the Tree of Knowledge of Good and Evil and brought the Fall upon the entire family of man. Elder Christofferson taught, "But with the Fall, both they and we gain sufficient knowledge and understanding to be enticed by good and evil—we attain a state of accountability and can recognize the alternatives before us" ("Moral Agency"). Agency requires knowledge.

Adam and Eve would either continue to live forever in their current state (2 Nephi 2:22), or partake of the fruit and experience death. They were subject to the laws governing their realm and the consequences outlined by that law. Moral agency does not work in chaos. If consequences to choices were not affixed by law, then there would be no need or purpose to choosing. Imagine again the restaurant with only one item on the menu. It doesn't matter what you order, you always get the same result. Now imagine a restaurant where you order the filet mignon and they bring you macaroni and cheese. Without fixed, predictable consequences to our choices, our choices have no meaning.

We sometimes fail to understand that the freedom to choose our actions does not mean that we are free to choose the consequences of our actions. Elder Christofferson taught, "Freedom of choice is the freedom to obey or disobey existing laws—not the freedom to alter their consequences. Law, as mentioned earlier, exists as a foundational element of moral agency with fixed outcomes that do not vary according to our opinions or preferences" ("Moral Agency"). Agency requires consequences fixed by law.

All four elements of agency—freedom to choose, alternatives, knowledge, and consequences—were present in the Garden of Eden, but until the Fall, they would not be available to the rest of the family of man. Adam and Eve lived in a paradisiacal and paradoxical state. They could not enjoy all the blessings of agency without disobedience (transgression), and they could not disobey without agency.

Lucifer, the Son of the Morning who had been cast down (Isaiah 14:12), took it upon himself to thwart the plan of God by tempting Adam and Eve to eat of the fruit of the Tree of Knowledge of Good and Evil. He thought that by convincing Adam and Eve to transgress the commandments of God that he would subvert Heavenly Father's plan. He tempted Eve by telling her, "Ye shall not surely die; For God doth know that in the day ye eat thereof, then your eyes shall be opened, and ye shall be as gods, knowing good and evil" (Moses 4:10–11). How ironic! Here is Lucifer, who tried to destroy the agency of man, using the lure of knowledge and agency to convince Adam and Eve to transgress God's command. With perhaps a partial understanding of what was at stake, Eve partook of the forbidden fruit. She then convinced Adam to also partake. Through the power of choice, Adam and Eve set in motion Heavenly Father's plan of happiness.

After they were cast out of the Garden of Eden, Adam and Eve suffered the consequences of their choice. They were now mortal and would eventually die, along with all of their posterity, but they were also now capable of having posterity. Eve expressed it well when she said, "Were it not for our transgression we never should have had seed, and never should have known good and evil, and the joy of our redemption, and the eternal life which God giveth unto all the obedient" (Moses 5:11). Because of Adam and Eve's transgression, every soul that came to earth would be free to choose their own spiritual destiny.

Cain was one of those souls. The story of his murderous act has always seemed out of place to me. Why would we want to spend so much time discussing someone that killed his brother to get gain? Because the story of Cain is a powerful illustration of personal choice and an example of how God seldom interferes with the agency of man, even when it adversely affects another human being. The story of Cain and Abel teaches us more about agency than a thousand sermons because Cain and Abel represent each of us.

Cain was born to good parents who loved him. When he was born, Eve said, "I have gotten a man from the Lord" (Moses 5:16). She and her husband taught their children the gospel, but Cain "hearkened not, saying, 'Who is the Lord that I should know him?'" (Moses 5:16). Cain exercised his agency and chose not to hearken to the teachings of his righteous parents, or to the Lord, and that choice caused him to fall out of favor with God.

Abel was Cain's younger brother. Just like Cain, Abel was taught by righteous parents. But unlike Cain, Abel "hearkened unto the voice of the Lord" (Moses 5:17). Abel exercised his agency and chose to listen to the teachings of his parents and the voice of the Lord (the Spirit). This choice led him to offer an acceptable sacrifice unto the Lord, and he was blessed of God.

Cain also offered a sacrifice, not out of obedience to God, but out of obedience to Satan. "And Cain loved Satan more than God. And Satan commanded him, saying: Make an offering unto the Lord" (Moses 5:18). The Lord rejected Cain's sacrifice, and in the process rebuked and counseled this rebellious soul in an attempt to bring him to repentance. The Lord said unto Cain, "If thou doest well, thou shalt be accepted. And if thou doest not well, sin lieth at the door, and Satan desireth to have thee; and except thou shalt hearken unto my commandments, I will deliver thee up" (Moses 5:23). All the conditions of agency were in place. Cain had the power to choose. He had alternatives to choose between. (In this case complete opposites.) He had knowledge, both of God and of Satan. His choice would bring consequences upon his head. Cain was empowered by agency to determine his own fate.

In *East of Eden*, the classic novel by John Steinbeck, the Chinese servant, Lee, embarks on a study of the story of Cain in an attempt to understand and explain it to his employer, Adam. At first he is confused at the wording in the Bible. It seemed that one translation predestined Cain to his fate and the other translation forced Cain to obey. After several years of study, Lee takes the matter to a group of "ancient reverend gentlemen" in hopes that they will enlighten him. Together they turned to the Hebrew text for clarification and after two years of study came to an understanding.

Their understanding hinged on one Hebrew word. Lee explained, "But the Hebrew word, the word *tim-shel*—'Thou mayest'—that gives a choice. It might be the most important word in the world. That says the way is open. That throws it right back on the man. For if 'Thou mayest'—it is also true that 'Thou mayest not.' Don't you see?" Lee celebrated this understanding, declaring that the power to choose, "Why, that makes a man great, that gives him stature with the gods." He exclaimed, "But think of the glory of the choice! That makes a man a man" (*East of Eden*, 301). The power to choose makes the human soul divine.

Cain had the power to choose his destiny just as Abel did. He was not forced to listen to the voice of the Lord, but he was invited to. He was not forced to listen to Satan, but he chose to. He was not forced to offer up an unacceptable sacrifice, but with the encouragement of Satan, he gathered the unworthy fruit of the field and offered it anyway. When he was rebuked of the Lord, he was not forced to change his ways, but the consequences of the choice before him were explained. Satan did not force Cain to slay his brother Abel. Cain exercised his agency and made an unrighteous choice and suffered consequences so severe because of his choice that he complained, "My punishment is greater than I can bear" (Genesis 4:13).

How often are we like Cain? We are given the gift of agency, the power to choose. We have alternatives to choose between. We are taught the truth and have the knowledge necessary to choose. We are called to repentance by a loving Heavenly Father who explains the consequences that will come if we choose not to follow His laws. We are invited to be obedient, but we love Satan's temptations more than God's laws. Then, when God's justice is brought to bear in our life and we begin to experience the consequences of our choices, we complain that the punishment is too harsh. However, like Cain, our complaining and protesting is misplaced. Because we have been given agency, along with the requisite alternatives and knowledge, we have complete control over the consequences. If we wish to complain to someone, we need to look in the mirror, not at God. We are the masters of our own destiny.

Lehi taught, "Wherefore, men are free according to the flesh; and all things are given them which are expedient unto man. And they are free to choose liberty and eternal life, through the great Mediator of all men, or to choose captivity and death, according to the captivity and power of the devil; for he seeketh that all men might be miserable like unto himself" (2 Nephi 2:27). Satan succeeded at fooling Cain into choosing to be miserable like he was.

Perhaps we should do away with personal agency. After all, decision-making is risky and fraught with danger. We might make the wrong choice and wind up in consequences we don't want. We might rebel like Cain and become a spiritual vagabond suffering for eternity. Why can't we simply be forced to do what is right so that we can all enjoy the blessings promised to the obedient? This, of course, was Lucifer's plan. He wanted to destroy the agency of man (Moses 4:3). But would his plan work? Could we be saved without agency? Could we be exalted without agency?

What is Heavenly Father's plan for us? He wants to "bring about the immortality and eternal life of man" (Moses 1:39). He wants us to become like Him. What is He like? He is omnipotent, in other words, all-powerful. He is omniscient, or all-knowing. He loves unconditionally. He is just and merciful. He has the ultimate freedom, and ability, to act instead of being acted upon. If we are to become like Him then we cannot accept the inert condition of simply being acted upon or forced to behave a certain way. Take away the ability to choose and you take away the power and ability of God.

By seeking to destroy the agency of man and also take upon himself the glory of the Father, Satan was using the ultimate circular argument. He would use godlike force to compel God's children to obey and then he would be crowned with the glory of God for doing so. He would become a god by being a god. No messy choices to deal with. No laws to obey. No necessity to exercise faith. No need to repent. He promised that all of us would become like our Father in Heaven, the ultimate free agent in the universe, by *not* acting at all. It was the lie at the heart of Satan's plan that fooled a third of the hosts of heaven.

Imagine that Heavenly Father's plan of happiness is like an airplane—maybe even the F-16 Fighting Falcon. It has a powerful engine, state-of-the-art avionics, efficient wings, and a plush cockpit. It is capable of soaring to great heights and reaching speeds over twice the speed of sound. It can perform nimble acrobatic stunts and roar into the sky like a rocket. It is a marvelous piece of engineering! How well would it work without any jet fuel? Without fuel it is nothing more than an expensive and intricate ghost of a machine incapable of flight. Agency is the fuel that makes God's plan of happiness work.

Not a single principle or ordinance of the gospel will work without agency. Faith must be chosen and exercised freely without compulsion. Repentance requires the choice of a willing heart. All ordinances are ineffective if they are performed by compulsion. Every commandment obeyed, every covenant made, and every prayer uttered requires the participant to choose. Compulsory faith is not faith; it is brainwashing. Forced obedience is not obedience; it is servitude. A covenant compelled has no power to exalt. Agency is the fuel that drives the plan of salvation. Without moral agency, the gospel carries no energy to save—let alone exalt. Even though God can offer us the gift of immortality, He cannot exalt us (give us eternal life) without our choosing. He cannot carry out His work or His glory without first giving us the ability to disobey Him.

Nothing ennobles the human spirit and makes humankind more godlike than the power of choice.

Using Our Agency Effectively

If the power to direct our life and choose our own destiny is one of God's greatest gifts, then why do we seem to make such poor choices? Why do we abuse our moral agency by making choices that disappoint our Heavenly Father who granted us agency in the first place? We sing the words, "Choose the right when a choice is placed before you," (*Hymns*, no. 239), but every week we are back at the sacrament table repenting for the wrong choices we have made. Why do we do this?

Of course we aren't alone in this dilemma. The scriptures are full of saints who were also sinners. Several stalwart prophets have lamented their weakness when it comes to sin. Nephi proclaimed, "O wretched man that I am! Yea, my heart sorroweth because of my flesh; my soul grieveth because of mine iniquities. I am encompassed about, because of the temptations and the sins which do so easily beset me. And when I desire to rejoice, my heart groaneth because of my sins" (2 Nephi 4:17–19). This of course is the same Nephi that told his doubting brothers, "If God had commanded me to do all things I could do them. If he should command me that I should say unto this water, be thou earth, it should be earth; and if I should say it, it would be done" (1 Nephi 17:50). If Nephi had trouble choosing the right all the time, then perhaps we aren't alone in our efforts to use our agency effectively.

Peter understood and believed in the divinity of Jesus Christ. When asked, "But whom say ye that I am?" (Matthew 16:16). Peter answered, "Thou art the Christ, the Son of the living God" (Matthew 12:16). Peter's conviction was strengthened by his experience on the Mount of Transfiguration where he witnessed a transfigured Jesus, Moses, and Elias and heard the voice of God the Father (Matthew 17). Yet in spite of his multiple miraculous witnesses, Peter would deny Christ three times during the night that Christ was betrayed. Why wasn't he able to remain faithful during that critical time? His weakness caused him sore repentance, and the scriptures record that he "wept bitterly" (Luke 22:62).

Why do we struggle to choose the right? Do we lack understanding of what is right and wrong? Probably not; since everyone is born with the Light of Christ and has an innate sense of right and wrong, most people have a built-in understanding of right and wrong (Moroni 7:18). Is it a lack of desire? Maybe for some people, but the nature of most people is to behave according to general law and order. The worldwide average number of law enforcement officers per one hundred thousand people hovers at around three hundred (Wikipedia, "List of Countries and Dependencies by Number of Police Officers"). In general, people are law-abiding and obedient.

When I was young, we lived in an old farmhouse located down a long gravel road almost a mile from the highway. When my parents would leave on some errand in town, they typically gave us small tasks or chores to perform—like putting away our toys or washing the dishes—before we were allowed to play or watch TV. It would have been easy to simply do the required chores before turning to recreation, but being typical children, we rarely did. Instead we posted a watchman at the window to look out for our parents' car to turn off the highway and onto our gravel road. Since the gravel road was almost a mile long that would give us time to hurry and finish whatever task our parents had assigned us before they left. Our plan worked well, except when our lookout failed. When that happened, Mom and Dad usually surprised us by walking through the front door unannounced to find us playing or watching TV and all the assigned tasks undone. The consequences of our disobedience were never pleasant, but we continued to do it anyway. It was easy to obey my parents when they were standing beside me, but it was even easier to *disobey* when they went away.

Before we came to earth and had a veil placed over our spiritual memory, we lived with our Father in Heaven. We didn't need faith in Him. We *knew* Him. This knowledge made exercising our agency easier. We felt our Father's love. We wanted to please Him. We wanted to be like him. Our proximity to Him made it easier for us to choose the right.

If Heavenly Father's work and glory is our immortality and eternal life, then this life is our opportunity to practice our agency and prove that we are worthy of His work and glory. We read in Abraham that this life is a time for Heavenly Father to "prove" us and see if we will do all things the Lord commands (Abraham 3:25). In other words, this life is a test. We had to leave the presence of our Father in Heaven in order for us to be tested. We had to be separated from Him for our agency to grow. We needed a proving and training ground that allowed us the opportunity to choose for ourselves and to learn from our own experience how to use our agency to its full potential.

So here we are, in the perfect environment for learning to exercise our agency. We have the freedom to choose, a world full of alternatives, ample knowledge, and unavoidable consequences for the choices we make. It is a wonderful plan! The only problem is that the consequences of our choices can be severe. In other words, we know what is right and wrong, but like Peter, we still fail to live up to the level of our knowledge. What we *know* and what we *do* are not in harmony, but the only way to bring them into harmony is by practice and training.

The world of aviation has a similar problem. Aviation is not inherently dangerous, but it can be unforgiving of error, and the outcome of error can be catastrophic—even deadly. Yet successful aviators cannot gain the skills necessary to succeed without trial and error. Knowledge is not enough; skills must be practiced. To develop good aeronautical decision-making skills, pilots must make poor aeronautical decisions and live to tell about them. You become a better pilot if you survive your mistakes. It is an effective way of learning, but risky, inefficient, and costly.

To solve this problem, Edwin Link, a barnstorming pilot of the 1920s, invented and patented the first flight simulator—"The Pilot Maker"—in 1929. Flight schools weren't interested at first and his invention ended up as a carnival ride, but when WWII began, the military employed his simulators to increase the survival rate of their student pilots. Simulation has been a hallmark of aviation ever since. We can apply the same principle to learning to exercise our agency properly.

How do we make the most of life experiences without risking a deadly mistake? How can we make the most of our opportunities to exercise agency without catastrophic failure? We must do what aviation professionals do. If we wish to use our agency effectively, we must practice and train to use our agency more effectively in a safe environment.

Years ago as a new Air Force pilot in training, I was subjected to a training technique called "the Emergency Procedures (EP) standup." We started our flying day standing at attention when the instructors entered the room. After a short greeting from our flight commander and maybe a few administrative announcements, one of the instructor pilots conducted emergency procedures training in the form of an oral evaluation in front of all the students and instructors. The instructor typically started by presenting a scenario. "You are flying in the practice area in straight and level flight at eight thousand feet when you notice that the oil pressure in your number two engine is zero." After a short pause, letting the facts settle over the nervous room, the instructor would call out the name of a student and state, "You have the aircraft."

The student pilot would stand up and begin to tell the instructor (with his or her classmates and all the other instructors watching and listening) how to handle the situation. The student would have to recite any steps that were to be conducted by memory and then appropriately apply any emergency checklists, procedures, or knowledge of aircraft systems to bring the scenario to a safe and logical conclusion. If the student failed to talk through the scenario and arrive at a safe and acceptable conclusion, he or she would be grounded for the day and receive a negative write-up in his or her grade book.

It was a harrowing experience! Students' hands would shake. Voices would crack. Beads of sweat

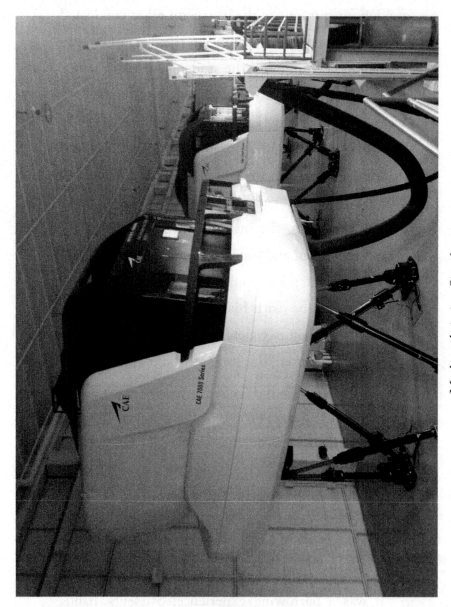

Modern Aviation Simulator

would sometimes break out on foreheads. Stomachs would tie up in knots. Why did the instructors make this so stressful every morning? This artificial stress placed on the students helped prepare them for the real event. The instructors wanted to ensure that if the students ever faced a real emergency in the airplane, they were prepared with knowledge and armed with good decision-making skills. They wanted to give the students the benefit of experience without the risk of the actual experience.

In addition to verbally testing students with emergency scenarios, the curriculum also called for training in simulators. Much like the simulators first invented by Edwin Link, the modern simulator allowed for an instructor to simulate flight conditions before the student actually flew. In addition to simulating everyday flight conditions and practicing normal procedures, the simulator also provided a format for training students on abnormal and emergency procedures that were too dangerous to practice in real life. It was a golden opportunity to have experience before the actual life lesson. It provided instructors a way to test student pilots without risking their lives.

Ejection is dangerous, even when things work like they are supposed to. It is too risky (and expensive) for student pilots to actually eject during the learning process. Student pilots learn to execute an ejection properly by using multiple simulation devices. They practice the proper body position in a mock-up cockpit, or an ejection seat attached to a large hydraulic piston. They practice the post-ejection checklist and dealing with parachute malfunctions using a hanging harness to simulate what it would be like under the actual parachute. They practice the parachute landing by jumping from a small platform into a sandy pit. They practice steering the parachute and landing by parasailing behind a truck or boat. They watch instructional videos on the ejection decision. They spend time in the simulator facing possible ejection scenarios. They spend hours with their instructors discussing the ejection decision.

One specific example of this type of preparation is rehearsing the ejection decision if the aircraft is in an uncontrollable spin. During an uncontrollable spin the aircraft is falling at around six thousand feet per minute. The ground is spinning around and around in the windshield. Often the centrifugal forces pin the pilot against the side of the cockpit making it difficult to sit upright. Because the aircraft is falling at such a high rate, the parachute won't have time to open and decelerate the pilot's fall before impact with the ground, and the rocket motors in the ejection seat cannot guarantee a safe ejection below a certain altitude. Without preparation, deciding when to eject would be a difficult—almost impossible—decision. Imagine a pilot in a spinning aircraft hurtling toward the ground trying to do a mathematical calculation based on how fast he is falling and the capabilities of the rocket motors in the ejection seat to determine at what altitude he must initiate the ejection in order to survive. The odds of making the right decision in the heat of the moment are slim.

Now imagine instead that a pilot has pulled out the performance charts of the ejection seat while she is on the ground in the squadron ready room. She can take her time and look at terrain charts to determine how it might affect her decision. She can do the mathematical calculations considering the sink rate of the airplane, her reaction time, and the capabilities of the ejection seat rocket motors while sitting comfortably at her desk. She can consider the various acrobatic maneuvers individually and come up with a predetermined altitude for initiating the ejection if things go wrong. Armed with this thorough preparation, she greatly reduces the risk for error and increases her odds for survival in the real situation.

Ejection is dangerous, but not as dangerous as crashing the airplane. Student pilots must have enough training on the ground to make the ejection decision in the air an automatic one. They have to learn to recognize the conditions that warrant an ejection and make the decision to eject *before* they ever strap into the airplane. Making that decision ahead of time can save their lives.

Can we apply these same principles and techniques to help us learn how to exercise our agency properly? Can we arm ourselves with information that will help us choose the right when the choice is placed before us? Can we practice choosing the right, or better yet, can we make some of the more risky decisions ahead of time—like pilots do—instead of in the heat of the moment? Yes, we can! Not only are we able to do this, but according to a prophet of God, we *should* do it.

Spencer W. Kimball taught, "Now may I make a recommendation? Develop discipline of self so that, more and more, you do not have to decide and re-decide what you will do when you are confronted with the same temptation time and time again. You only need to decide some things *once!* How great a blessing it is to be free of agonizing over and over again regarding a temptation. To do such is time-consuming and very risky.

"Likewise, my dear young friends, the positive things you will want to accomplish need only be decided upon once—like going on a mission and living worthily in order to get married in the temple—and then all other decisions related to these goals can fall into line. Otherwise, each consideration is risky, and each equivocation may result in error. There are some things Latter-day Saints do, and other things we just don't do. The sooner you take stands, the taller you will be!" ("President Kimball Speaks Out on Planning Your Life").

Like the fighter pilot, we can—and should—make some of the more risky decisions ahead of time and not in the heat of the moment. We must prepare to make good decisions. If we wish to use our agency effectively, we must *train* to use our agency more effectively.

The Emergency Checklist

In all situations—

✓ **Maintain Aircraft Control**

- At all times—fly the airplane

✓ **Analyze the Situation**

- Use your knowledge of aircraft systems to analyze the problem

✓ **Take Appropriate Action**

- Execute the emergency procedures

✓ **Land as Soon as Conditions Permit**

- Get the aircraft safely on the ground

The Agency Checklist

In all situations—

✓ **Maintain Agency Control**

- At all times—keep your agency

✓ **Analyze the Choice**

- How will this decision affect my life?

- What decision will maintain my values?

- Have I made this decision already?

✓ **Exercise Your Agency Appropriately**

- Choose the right!

✓ **Get to Safety as Soon as Conditions Permit**

- Put yourself in a "safe" environment

- Talk about your decision with a parent/mentor/leader

THE AGENCY CHECKLIST

Aircraft emergencies are similar to the difficult choices in life. Bad things happen. Machines break, and systems fail. What do pilots do when something goes wrong? They use checklists. But just like in life, not every emergency can be foreseen, and not every emergency has a specific checklist. Over the years, aviators have learned to rely on a few basic principles in every emergency situation. These life-saving tenets are committed to memory and used in all situations that arise.

Life does not come with a checklist, but we do have a few procedural manuals (the scriptures) we can learn from. We do have instructors (parents) and mentors (Church leaders) that can help and teach us. Perhaps we could apply an emergency checklist similar to the one used in aviation to help us effectively use our moral agency.

Let's look at how we could apply these principles when we are exercising our agency.

✓ MAINTAIN AIRCRAFT CONTROL

Fly the aircraft at all times. It may sound funny that the first step on a pilot's checklist is a reminder to fly the airplane, but many accidents and many lives have been lost because the pilot simply stopped flying the aircraft. The most famous accident of this type was Eastern Airlines Flight 401, an L1011 that crashed into the Florida Everglades on December 29, 1972, and killed over one hundred people, including the entire crew. As the aircraft lined up for landing, the crew extended the landing gear. The nose gear light (a small light in the cockpit that indicates that the gear is in the proper position for landing) did not illuminate. The captain directed a go-around and the cockpit crew began to analyze the problem. While they were analyzing and trying to fix the problem, the aircraft descended and crashed into the swampy everglades ("Accident Reports," AAR7314).

What was the root cause of the accident? Nobody was flying the aircraft. The first officer engaged the

autopilot, but for some reason (perhaps because someone bumped the control yoke while they were trying
to resolve the problem) the autopilot disengaged. No
warning sounded. Without a member of the cockpit
crew flying the airplane, it descended and crashed.

The first rule for dealing with any situation in the
airplane is Maintain Aircraft Control.

✓ Maintain Agency Control

Never give up control of your agency. Consider
Heavenly Father's plan. He never requires us to abandon our agency. He invites us to follow His plan of
our own free will and choice. The hymn, "Know This,
That Every Soul Is Free" (*Hymns*, no. 240) describes it
well. God will allow each of us to choose what we'll
be. He will "call, persuade, direct aright." He will bless
us with "wisdom, love, and light." But He will "never
force the human mind."

Agency is essential to Heavenly Father's plan for
us and He will never ask us to abandon our free will.
He allows us to maintain our agency at all times, but
He does invite, persuade, and encourage us to exercise our agency in accordance with His laws because
He knows we will be happy if we do. To each law He
has attached a consequence, albeit blessing or curse.

"There is a law, irrevocably decreed in heaven before the foundations of this world, upon which all blessings are predicated—and when we obtain any blessing from God, it is by obedience to that law upon which it is predicated" (D&C 130:20–21). Heavenly Father endowed each of us with the gift of agency. Without that gift we would not be responsible for our choices or the consequences of our choices. Heavenly Father will never take away our agency.

Satan, on the other hand, will attempt to subvert our agency and trap us. Heavenly Father cast him out of His presence because he attempted to "destroy the agency of man" (Moses 4:3), and he has been trying to destroy that agency ever since. Consider all the trap-like temptations that he uses to pervert the use of our agency—drug addiction, alcohol addiction, pornography, lying, and sexual promiscuity. With each sin we commit, we give up some of our agency and allow ourselves to be bound by spiritual—and sometimes even physical—chains. What at first appears to be a liberating experience used to cast off all restrictions and live a "free" life soon becomes a jail cell where we are no longer in charge of our own choices. Sin causes our agency to shrink, and eventually we will find ourselves to be slaves instead of masters. In the end, Satan "will not support his children at the last day, but doth speedily drag them down to hell" (Alma 30:60).

What can we do to maintain our agency? First we have to acknowledge that we are responsible for our choices. We cannot use the cop-out excuse that "the devil made me do it." We must accept we are the masters of our own destiny and not simply products of our environment. We cannot maintain our agency if we don't recognize ourselves as the masters of our own fate.

Next we must guard against anything and anyone that might try to take away our agency. We cannot abdicate our agency to peer pressure, popular opinion, or predatory advertising. We must resist the urge to follow the crowd, especially when we know the crowd is going the wrong direction. We should be careful to maintain our individual agency when we feel pressured to do something because everyone is doing it.

We should be wary of any program that promises reward without personal responsibility or individual agency. If we are not careful, well-intentioned programs or well-disguised traps will limit our ability to choose. Laws should be framed that "will secure to each individual the free exercise of conscience, the right and control of property, and the protection of life"

(D&C 134:2). Laws are necessary to protect individual safety, property, and the common good, but they should not limit our moral agency. Legal authorities "should restrain crime, but never control conscience; should punish guilt, but never suppress the freedom of the soul" (D&C 134:4). David O. McKay said, "Any form of government that destroys or undermines the free exercise of free agency is wrong." ("Free Agency," 87).

Heavenly Father endowed each of us with life and also the power to direct that life. He establishes laws and affixes consequences to actions, but He will not force obedience, extort faith, or demand compliance. He will invite, inspire, and encourage. He will allow us to suffer the consequences of our choices. We can give away our agency, but He will *never* take our agency from us.

If we wish to exercise our agency appropriately, we must first maintain our agency and carefully guard our right to choose.

✓ ANALYZE THE SITUATION

While keeping the aircraft flying safely, pilots must analyze the malfunction or situation. They must use their knowledge of aircraft systems, aerodynamics, and procedural knowledge to identify the problem. They may have to do some troubleshooting or refer to a schematic in order to properly understand what is going on with the airplane. Perhaps a generator has failed, or a hydraulic system has overheated. A correct analysis is essential to solving the problem. (Pilots have shut down functioning systems and even working engines because they misdiagnosed the problem.) Simple malfunctions have defined checklists for handling them, but a rushed or incorrect analysis could prove fatal, or at least embarrassing.

To help analyze inflight malfunctions, pilots first attend ground school. They learn about the various aircraft systems—hydraulics, engines, avionics, fuel, and so on—and the possible malfunctions. They learn about the myriad warning or status lights in the cockpit and what they each mean. They study schematics to better understand the inner workings of the aircraft they will be flying. Not only do they study, they are also required to pass an exam proving that they have a basic knowledge of the machine before they are qualified to take it into the air. With that preparation, when trouble arises in the air they are able to properly analyze it, and with proper analysis, correct action can be taken.

On July 19, 1989, United Airlines Flight 232 was cruising at an altitude of thirty-seven thousand feet on its way to Denver, Colorado. It had been an uneventful flight in the DC-10 until the cockpit crew heard a loud bang and felt the aircraft shudder and vibrate. They looked at the engine instruments and could see that the tail-mounted engine had experienced catastrophic failure. They began the appropriate emergency checklist but soon realized that the aircraft was difficult to control, an abnormality for a simple engine failure. Upon further analysis, they recognized that the aircraft hydraulic system (a system of high pressure pumps and actuators that move the primary flight controls, secondary flight controls, and landing gear) had also failed. Drawing on their systems knowledge, they employed the standby hydraulic pump, but to no avail. Working together they used the thrust from the engines to control the airplane. The captain solicited the help of a training check airman (a pilot qualified to train and evaluate other pilots in the aircraft) who happened to be riding in the back of the aircraft. With the captain working the controls in conjunction with the first officer, and the check airman on his knees making constant adjustments to the engine thrust levers, they managed to maintain control of the aircraft. Using all of their combined skill and knowledge, they made an emergency landing at a small airfield in Sioux City, Iowa. The aircraft cartwheeled upon landing. Over one hundred people were killed and many more seriously injured. But when the accident was analyzed, investigators determined that the aircraft should not have been able to fly at all. The skill and knowledge of the aircrew saved the lives of hundreds through proper analysis and application of knowledge ("Human Factors in Aviation Maintenance").

The second step—Analyze the situation.

✓ ANALYZE THE CHOICE

"Choose the right when a choice is placed before you" (*Hymns*, no. 239). It sounds simple enough, but how do we know what is right when the choice is placed before us? *How will the decision affect my life? What decision will maintain my values?* Perhaps we must do like the professional pilot and prepare to make the right choice through preparation and study *before* the choice is placed before us.

Just like pilots, we have a variety of resources to help us analyze the choice before us. We have the scriptures. Just imagine—thousands of years of inspiration and wisdom abridged and encapsulated into a resource of a few hundred pages. What an amazing tool! Through the scriptures, we can learn from the mistakes of others. We can get inspiration from the courage of those who came before us who have faced difficult choices. We can build faith from the miracles of others. We can learn about the consequences of a variety of choices by studying the outcome of others choices, both individually and as societies. The scriptures can help us analyze the choices we will face before we face them.

Modern prophets and seers can help us analyze the choices before us. We know "the Lord God will do nothing, but he revealeth his secret unto his servants the prophets" (Amos 3:7). Modern prophets receive revelation for our day. In addition to being prophets, they are also seers. From the Book of Mormon we know "that a seer is greater than a prophet," and "that a seer is a revelator and a prophet also; and a gift which is greater can no man have" (Mosiah 8:15–16). Like the name implies, modern-day seers have the ability to "see" into the future. A modern seer then can teach, guide, and warn us to keep us on the right path and away from danger. What an incredible resource to help us analyze the variety of choices we face! Modern-day prophets and seers can help us with our analysis of difficult choices before we face them.

In addition to prophets and seers, we also have local leaders to help us with difficult choices. Stake presidents, bishops, Sunday School teachers, youth leaders, home teachers, visiting teachers, and parents all stand ready to help us analyze the choices we face. They have the advantage of experience that we can draw upon. Likewise, priesthood leaders posses priesthood keys that entitle them to inspiration on our behalf. Sunday School teachers and youth leaders have been called and set apart specifically to help teach us and are also entitled to guidance and inspiration. We have so many loving members of the Church that stand ready to guide us in our choices. Like Heavenly Father, they do not want to control us, but want to keep us safe from the dangers of poor choices.

One Sunday in sacrament meeting, I watched a toddler crawl up the aisle toward the front of the chapel. The parents watched but did not intervene yet. An elderly brother sitting near the front of the chapel saw the child crawling by. Instead of waiting on the parents, or sitting there annoyed at the distraction, he lovingly picked up the crawler and turned him around, and the toddler crawled back to his parents. He didn't stop the child from crawling or restrict his movement. He simply turned him around. This is exactly what our parents and leaders want to do for us. They want to turn us around when we are headed into danger. They don't want to control us or take our agency, but they do want to see us moving in the right direction. We would be wise to heed their direction.

We are all born with a powerful gift to help us analyze the choices before us and shine divine light on the decision. "For behold, the Spirit of Christ is given to every man, that he may know good from evil" (Moroni 7:16). We are born with this powerful gift of spiritual discernment and are admonished, "And now, my brethren, seeing that ye know the light by which ye may judge, which light is the light of Christ, see that ye do not judge wrongfully" (Moroni 7:16). The Light of Christ can guide us and help us analyze the choices before us.

In addition to the Light of Christ, the Holy Ghost will also guide us in our decision-making. "And by the power of the Holy Ghost ye may know the truth of all things" (Moroni 10:5). Think about it. A member of the Godhead stands ready to testify and teach of the truth of all things if we are willing to listen. When we seek the confirmation of the Holy Ghost, He will "enlighten your mind," and "shall fill your soul with joy" (D&C 11:13). The Holy Ghost, like a good co-pilot, can be our constant companion and can help us in times of crisis, but if we give Him the opportunity, He can help us choose between right and wrong before we are faced with a difficult choice. The Holy Ghost is an invaluable resource for exercising our agency appropriately.

With all these tools and resources at our disposal, how could we go wrong? Robert D. Hales spoke of an experience he had in pilot training. One of his class-mates, an all-American football player, ignored the resources available to teach and train him, and when the time came for making a critical decision, he was unprepared.

> When it came time for him to go to the trainer to learn emergency procedures and to precon-dition his mental and physical responses so that they would be automatic, even instanta-neous, this all-American would put his arm around the instructor and say, 'Check me off for three hours of emergency procedure.' Then, instead of training, he would go to the swimming pool, pistol range, or to the golf

course. Later in the training the instructor said to him, 'What are you going to do when there is an emergency and you are not prepared?' His answer, 'I am never going to bail out; I am never going to have an emergency.' He never learned the emergency procedures which he should have mastered in preparatory training.

A few months later, on an evening mission, fire erupted in the quiet sky over Texas. The fire-warning light lit up. When the plane dropped to 5,000 feet in flames, the young pilot who was with him said, 'Let's get out of here.' And, with centrifugal force pulling against him, the young man who took his training seriously struggled to get out of the airplane and bailed out. His parachute opened at once. And he slammed to the ground. He received serious injuries but survived.

My friend who had not felt the need to train stayed with the airplane and died in the crash. He paid the price for not having learned the lessons that could have saved his life. ("The Aaronic Priesthood: Return with Honor")

Just like pilots that do not prepare and train for emergencies, we also risk making poor choices if we don't analyze some decisions ahead of time and prepare to execute our decision automatically. Difficult and weighty decisions are much easier to analyze in a quiet moment of reflection surrounded by information and inspired by the Holy Ghost than in the noisy and chaotic moment with peer pressure weighing on our shoulders and Satan screaming in our ears.

Many difficult decisions can and should be thoroughly analyzed and decided beforehand. Just like the fighter pilot who has studied the various ejection scenarios so that when he is faced with the decision he will not waver or hesitate to save his life, you can also protect yourself from deadly hesitation or vacillation. Then when you are faced with one of these difficult and risky choices you simply need to ask yourself one question—*Have I a made this decision already?*

Take time *now* to study and analyze a variety of choices *before* you are faced with them. You can calmly analyze important choices like: Should I view pornography? Is it okay to have sex before marriage? What will happen if I drink alcohol? Are drugs really harmful? Should I pay an honest tithe?

Investigate these difficult choices beforehand using the various resources available to you. Take time to ponder where your decisions might lead. Talk to your parents and leaders. Study the scriptures for inspiration. Meditate and listen to the Light of Christ. Seek the guidance of the Holy Ghost. This agency preparation and training will save you time, trouble, and risk, and just like Captain Stricklin, it will ensure a more favorable outcome in a dangerous situation.

✓ TAKE APPROPRIATE ACTION

Most emergency situations do not resolve themselves. Action is required. Now that the problem or situation has been properly analyzed, the pilot must take action to resolve it. Sometimes when the situation is time critical, she must apply quick action strictly from memory without referencing a checklist. If the situation does not require immediate action, an emergency checklist is available to methodically guide her through the necessary steps. If an emergency checklist or procedure for handling the problem does not exist, she must rely on her skills and experience to determine the appropriate course of action. In any case, the pilot cannot be passive. She must act to save the aircraft, the crew, and the passengers.

On July 6, 2013, Asiana Flight 214, a Boeing 777, lined up for visual approach to runway 28L in San Francisco. The ten-hour flight from Seoul, Korea, carrying 293 passengers and 16 crewmembers had been uneventful up to that point. The aircraft was in perfect working order. It was a clear and sunny day with adequate visibility in the San Francisco Bay area. The only thing inoperative was the glideslope signal of the Instrument Landing System for the chosen runway, which helps the pilot maintain the correct descent angle as the aircraft approaches the runway, but the visual glideslope indicators were working normally. All factors indicated that the approach and landing would be a routine visual approach to successful landing, but it didn't end that way.

Although he had several thousand hours of flying time in large commercial aircraft, it was the captain's first visual approach in the B-777. The pilot acting as the first officer was an experienced training captain along to help the new captain learn the ropes of the new aircraft. Because the glideslope signal was out of service, they were late to begin their final descent and were above the normal glidepath. The captain adjusted by lowering the nose and increasing the descent rate. The autothrottle system (a system to adjust and control thrust from the engines similar to a cruise control in a car) reverted to a mode that reduced the thrust to idle. At five hundred feet the aircraft was descending at twelve hundred feet per minute, more than the acceptable rate, and the airspeed was high because of the increased sink rate. The correct action would have been to go around and try the approach again. Instead the crew continued without changing anything.

With the thrust commanded at idle by the auto-throttles and the aircraft descending at an excessive rate for the condition, the visual glideslope indicators showed the cockpit crew that they were getting too low. The captain adjusted by pulling back on the yoke and raising the nose. This action helped arrest the sink rate, but the throttles were still in idle. Like a car trying to accelerate uphill without pushing on the accelerator, the aircraft began to get dangerously slow. Nobody in the cockpit took action. Like passive bystanders they watched the aircraft approach a stall condition just one hundred feet above the ground. Finally, they added power, but it was too late. Jet engines take time to accelerate and produce thrust. In a matter of seconds the B-777, free of mechanical defects, slammed into the seawall short of the runway.

The impact ripped off the tail of the airplane and ejected several flight attendants in the aft galley and two passengers that were not wearing their seatbelts. The aircraft slammed into the runway, spun around, and skidded to stop. The right engine burst into flames. As the fire spread, the frightened passengers began to evacuate the aircraft. Many were seriously injured. All were in shock. Fortunately only three passengers were killed.

Like most accidents, several factors contributed to the final result: fatigue at the end of a long flight, miscommunication in the cockpit, and misunderstanding of the autothrottle system. But what would have prevented the accident? Action. At any time either the captain or the training captain acting as the first officer, could have prevented the accident by pushing the throttles forward. Either of them had the skills and knowledge to turn off the automation and fly the airplane to a safe and uneventful landing. The cockpit crew watched the accident unfold before their eyes without taking any corrective action, and the results were deadly ("Accident Reports," AAR140).

But how does the pilot know what to do?

All aircraft are similar, but each aircraft (particularly complex aircraft) has specific limitations and idiosyncrasies that pilots must understand to safely fly them. When an aircraft is brought into service, the manufacturer develops the emergency procedures. These procedures typically include procedural steps that must be committed to and executed from memory. When learning to fly a new aircraft, the pilot must commit any immediate action items to memory and then practice and rehearse them until their execution becomes automatic. Additionally, some procedural steps are less time critical and allow time for the pilot to reference a checklist. In order to execute the appropriate steps, the pilot must be familiar with and understand the consequences of each step in the checklist. Again, role-playing and simulation play an integral part in training a pilot on a new aircraft.

When an emergency situation occurs, the pilot must take appropriate action to resolve it.

✓ EXERCISE YOUR AGENCY APPROPRIATELY

All the preparation in the world will be worthless unless you act. When the moment of execution has arrived, the time for preparation has passed. Lehi taught, "Wherefore, the Lord God gave unto man that he should act for himself" (2 Nephi 2:16). We were divinely appointed to conduct our own lives and act for ourselves.

In the book of Revelation, the Lord counsels, "I know thy works, that thou art neither cold nor hot: I would thou wert cold or hot. So then because thou art lukewarm, and neither cold nor hot, I will spue thee out of my mouth" (Revelation 3:15–16). Who wants to be spewed out? What is wrong with being lukewarm? To understand the metaphor, we must think about the capabilities of hot and cold water. Hot water can cook, clean, and—if hot enough—even power things. Cold water can preserve, refresh, and chill. Both hot and cold water effect change on their immediate environment. Latter-day Saints have been instructed to be "agents unto themselves" (D&C 58:28). In other words, we should be change agents for good through our actions. When we fail to act, we are lukewarm and are indiscernible from our environment. The Lord expects us to make the world a better place, and if we are lukewarm, we can't do that.

Indecision in the moment of action comes in a variety of forms. Sometimes we fail to act because we are afraid of making a mistake. Maybe we fail to act because we are overwhelmed with information and can't decide what to do first. Perhaps we simply freeze up in a difficult situation because of stress. In any case, inaction at a critical moment can cost us spiritually and allow us to sin.

Action, preferably correct action, is essential in the moment of choice. Joseph of Egypt is a wonderful example of someone willing to take bold and correct action in a moment of decision. He had been sold into slavery by his older brothers and ended up in a nobleman's house. Potiphar, the nobleman, recognized Joseph's talents and put him in charge of his house— quite a compliment for young Hebrew slave. All was well until Potiphar's wife attempted to seduce Joseph. She made several sexual advances but he rebuffed her, saying, "How then can I do this great wickedness, and sin against God?" (Genesis 39:9).

Finally, one day she caught him in the house alone, and her advances became more aggressive. She grabbed his garment and insisted that he lie with her. How did Joseph respond? Did he consider the offer or hesitate in the moment of decision? No! He wasted no time and took action that would save his virtue. "He left his garment in her hand, and fled, and got him out" (Genesis 39:12). Joseph understood the need for correct action in the moment of decision and acted obediently to the commandments of God. Potiphar's wife lied about the encounter and had Joseph put into prison, but Joseph's quick action protected him from serious sin. Had he not acted quickly and obediently in that moment, no doubt the history of the entire Hebrew nation would be quite different today.

When the moment of execution has arrived, the time for preparation has passed. All the preparation in the world will be worthless unless you act. Choice requires action. Choosing the right will sometimes require bold action.

✓ LAND AS SOON AS CONDITIONS PERMIT

It is the hope of every pilot to end his flying career with the same number of landings as takeoffs. Flying is a magical experience, but crashing is a terrifying experience. When problems arise in flight, getting the aircraft safely on the ground is the pilot's ultimate goal, but rushing to land the aircraft can hinder that goal. Sometimes the safer course of action is to continue to fly until the aircraft is in a safe configuration to land. This requires discipline and patience on the part of the pilot. Sometimes the situation (like an uncontrollable fire) calls for an immediate landing before the aircraft is no longer capable of flight. In every case, getting the aircraft on the ground safely is the ultimate goal of each flight.

On January 31, 2000, around 1:30 in the afternoon, Alaska Airlines Flight 261 departed from Puerto Vallarta, Mexico, bound for San Francisco and Seattle. During the climb the aircraft experienced a problem with the flight controls. The jackscrew that controlled the elevator and pitch had jammed. The cockpit crew ran the appropriate checklist, and the aircraft was controllable. Nothing in the checklist specifically directed them to return to the departure airport and land, but the aircraft was capable of successfully landing at the departure airfield with the problem. The crew elected to continue the flight instead of returning to Puerto Vallarta. For almost the next two hours the aircraft flew without further problem, or at least it appeared that way. In reality, the mechanical failure became worse.

When they approached the United States border they radioed ahead and discussed the situation with their Dispatch and Maintenance Control. After deliberation, the cockpit crew elected to divert into Los Angeles. As they began to prepare for landing, the jackscrew failed completely. Without the elevator, the aircraft became uncontrollable and plunged from thirty-one thousand feet into the Pacific Ocean, killing everyone on board.

Several factors contributed to the decision to continue the flight, but if the cockpit crew had elected to land as soon as conditions permitted, they might have saved the aircraft and everyone on board. Instead they continued to fly with a significant problem and tried to troubleshoot it. The danger continued and eventually increased to the point of complete mechanical failure and a crash into the Pacific Ocean.

When faced with an airborne emergency or problem, land as soon as conditions permit.

✓ GET TO SAFETY AS SOON AS CONDITIONS PERMIT

Flirting with sin is a dangerous game. When we find ourselves in danger, we need to retreat to safety. Would we stay in a burning building? Would we swim at the edge of a powerful waterfall? Would we remain exposed to lightning during a thunderstorm? When we are surrounded by temptation, we must seek safety as soon as conditions permit if we wish to maintain our values and avoid the damaging effects of sin.

Captain Moroni understood this principle well. When faced with a powerful enemy, he readied his people for battle by preparing safe places of refuge and retreat. He prepared his people by "strengthening the armies of the Nephites, and erecting small forts, or places of resort; throwing up banks of earth round about to enclose his armies, and also building walls of stone to encircle them about, round about their cities and the borders of their lands; yea, all round about the land" (Alma 48:8). He knew that in order for them to win the war, they must have safe havens to protect them from harm.

What are our havens of protection and retreat from sin? First and foremost is a righteous home environment. We are commanded to "Organize yourselves; prepare every needful thing; and establish a house, even a house of prayer, a house of fasting, a house of faith, a house of learning, a house of glory, a house of order, a house of God" (D&C 88:119). Our homes should be a refuge from the storms of life and from the attacks of the adversary. Through prayer, fasting, and scripture study, we can do like Captain Moroni did and convert our homes into safe places of retreat.

The Church is designed to help and support families to live the gospel of Jesus Christ and is another fortification built to give us refuge from the destructive power of sin. In the Church we receive instruction, fellowship, and service that strengthen us against the temptations of the world and give us temporary respite from the evils that are prevalent in society. Not only is the Church a refuge, but it is also a spiritual hospital of sorts, mending our wounds through sacred ordinances. The Church can be a place of safety and protection.

Within the structure of the Church we have numerous people who stand ready to help us avoid and overcome sin. We have teachers, leaders, and other members to fellowship and serve us. We have members assigned as home teachers, visiting teachers, missionaries, and a host of other members in specific callings who stand ready to help us in any way they can. Most important, we have priesthood leaders who possess keys that can deliver us from spiritual bondage and help us more fully apply the Atonement in our lives. Bishops and stake presidents can help us recover from sin and help protect us from committing further sin by learning from our mistakes. The leaders, teachers, and members of the Church can provide a safe spiritual environment.

In addition to the chapels and meetinghouses of the Church, we have the sacred temples as places of retreat from spiritual danger. The prophet Isaiah described the temple as a "tabernacle for a shadow in the daytime from the heat, and for a place of refuge, and a covert from storm and from rain" (2 Nephi 14:6). This figurative language helps us to understand the spiritual peace we can find at the temple. President Monson also stated, "We are often surrounded by that which would drag us down. As you and I go to the holy houses of God, as we remember the covenants we make within, we will be more able to bear every trial and to overcome each temptation. In this sacred sanctuary we will find peace; we will be renewed and fortified" ("The Holy Temple, a Beacon to the World"). The holy temple is a safe place.

Perhaps our home is not a spiritual refuge, or we are away from home. Perhaps we cannot get to church or the temple right away. If we find ourselves alone and without a place of retreat in a moment of temptation or sin, we always have the Holy Ghost to guide us. When we are cut off from the immediate support of family members, friends, and Church leaders, we can always call upon heaven's help. Christ taught his disciples, "But the Comforter, which is the Holy Ghost, whom the Father will send in my name, he shall teach you all things, and bring all things to your remembrance, whatsoever I have said unto you" (John 14:26). President Eyring taught, "The companionship of the Holy Ghost makes what is good more attractive and temptation less compelling" ("The Holy Ghost as Your Companion"). In times of spiritual danger and temptation, we can always seek the comfort and guidance of the Holy Ghost.

Just like successful aviators, when we find ourselves in danger we must get to safety as soon as conditions permit, and likewise we should spend some time "debriefing" the event with a leader, friend, or mentor to help us capture the lessons learned from the experience, no matter what the outcome. After every mission or flight, professional aviators take a few minutes to discuss their performance and how they might improve. They try to reconstruct anything that went exceptionally well or particularly wrong and determine the root cause of the success or failure. Every attempt is made to capture the lessons learned so that any mistakes will not be repeated.

Once pilots are safely on the ground and the emergency situation terminated, they can discuss their actions with other pilots and how they could have done better. They can better analyze the root cause of the problem and determine how to better handle it in the future. Good pilots debrief their performance. When things don't go well and people get hurt or damage occurs, an accident investigation ensues in order to determine the causes and prevent future accidents. If their performance is not up to par, pilots are retrained, or sometimes even grounded from flying. In all cases, pilots must learn from their mistakes and hopefully from the mistakes of others.

The debrief is essential to aviation progress and safety. In fact, each of the incidents discussed in this book are available because of the thorough, investigative debriefing skills of pilots and accident investigators. This pattern of preparation, execution, and debriefing to capture the lessons learned has made aviation the safest mode of travel.

Discussing a difficult decision or a brush with temptation (even if the outcome was unsuccessful) helps us process the event and avoid future pitfalls and dangers. It also helps those with whom we share the experience learn vicariously through us. Additionally, we should write down the lessons learned in a journal. When faced with temptation and sin, get to safety as soon as possible. Take some time to discuss or "debrief" the event in order to capture the lessons learned from the experience.

In the case of Captain Stricklin, a safe landing with the aircraft was not possible. His only choices were to eject or die in the crash. Because of his extensive training, he recognized this and took the appropriate action—ejection. Even though the aircraft did not survive, *he did.*

When Orville and Wilbur Wright began flying and ushered the world into a new era, this emergency checklist did not exist. It was developed over time, but the cost was high. Each item of the checklist is written in the blood of one or more aviators that did not survive an emergency situation. Each principle of safety is built on the graves of pilots (and their passengers) that didn't follow them. The year 2014 was the safest year in the history of commercial aviation (Ranter, "Despite High Profile Accidents 2014 was the Safest Year Ever According to ASN Data"), but that safety was achieved through careful study of past errors and analysis of previous accidents. The rules of successful aviation are written in the blood of unsuccessful aviators. We can learn from their example, without having to repeat their deadly mistakes.

Life doesn't come with a checklist, but we do have the scriptures to teach us. We have Church leaders to guide and mentor us. We have the Holy Ghost to inspire us. Using our moral agency wisely will be one of the most difficult tasks of our lifetime. We can learn from our own mistakes, or we can glean from the wisdom and mistakes of those who have gone before.

AGENCY TRAINING

Flying in the weather requires the use of specialized instruments that provide the pilot with life-saving information. The attitude indicator, with an aircraft symbol and an artificial horizon, allows the pilot to keep the aircraft upright and to turn safely even when his vision is obscured by clouds or fog. The compass card tells the pilot which way the aircraft is flying. The radio beacons and GPS signals guide the aircraft to designated points in space. The altimeter tells the pilot how high above the earth the aircraft is. When the pilot can't see outside because of weather, the aircraft instruments can provide enough information for a properly trained pilot to navigate and steer the aircraft to a safe landing, even when thick fog obscures the runway and the visibility is almost zero.

In spite of the amazing technology in aircraft instruments, every year several pilots crash in marginal weather. Most of the time the accident investigation reveals that the aircraft instruments were working correctly, but for some reason the pilot did not follow the guidance provided. Was it a lack of training and understanding the instruments? Not usually. The mishap pilots are often knowledgeable and qualified. Was it a lack of desire to live? No; they were trying to safely land the aircraft. Was it lack of willpower or self-discipline? Perhaps. Pilot error is the most common cause for aircraft accidents, particularly in bad weather (planecrashinfo.com). They *knew* what to do. They *wanted* to do it. But what they *knew* and what they *did* were not in harmony.

Why do trained pilots who want to land safely in marginal weather crash because of pilot error? Often it is attributed to a phenomenon called spatial disorientation. Our bodies use several physical cues to discern and determine the attitude and performance of the aircraft. Experienced pilots can sense the acceleration, the climb, the descent, and the turn by using the "seat of their pants." The only problem is that those physical sensors can sometimes be fooled. When that happens, pilots may *think* they are in straight and level flight, when in reality they are in a turn. They may *feel* like they are climbing, when in reality they are descending. These spatial disorientation phenomena are so common and well-known that many have been given names: the leans, the giant hand, and the graveyard spiral. All of them can be deadly to a pilot that succumbs to the false cues that they give.

The most famous accident of this type is the fatal crash of John F. Kennedy Jr. While flying at night in marginal weather, he experienced the leans, which made him feel like he was turning when he was straight and level, or vice versa. He succumbed to this spatial disorientation and did the classic graveyard spiral into the Atlantic Ocean ("NTSB Releases Final Report on Investigation of Crash of Aircraft Piloted by John F. Kennedy Jr.").

Like aviators who have advanced instrumentation to guide them through the weather, we have the Holy Ghost as our spiritual instruments to guide us through clouds, thick fog, and bad weather to a safe landing. Like Air Traffic Controllers on the radio, we have leaders who can speak to us and steer us to a safe landing. If we want to stay on spiritual course, we must "take the Holy Spirit as *our* guide" (D&C 45:57) and follow the counsel of prophets. However, just like the pilots that succumb to spatial disorientation, we can also succumb to spiritual disorientation if we don't listen to the Holy Ghost.

How do pilots overcome the effects of spatial disorientation? They must be disciplined to trust the aircraft instrumentation instead of the physical cues. How do pilots learn to exercise that kind of discipline? They must practice and train in a safe environment. Professional pilots practice and train in order to overcome the erroneous physical cues and follow the guidance of the instruments.

If we are to find our way through the fog of life and use our agency effectively, we must do likewise. How can we train to use our agency? What does agency training look like? How do we prepare to act when the moment of decision is upon us? Life is too complex for us to foresee every decision and choice ahead of time. We don't always know which decisions will be difficult for us. However, we can prepare by following a few basic principles that will help us be better prepared in all situations.

One technique used effectively in aviation is scenario-based training or role-playing exercises. As mentioned before, Air Force pilots are subjected to a role-playing training technique called "the Emergency

Procedures (EP) Standup." Life is similar to that role-playing exercise. It is a giant "simulation" that allows us to practice using our agency and to be tested. We face challenging situations that stretch us and make us grow. Sometimes we fail and suffer the embarrassment of failure and defeat. Through it all we must keep trying to improve our performance.

How can we minimize the chance of failure and increase the chances for success at using our agency wisely? We can employ the same techniques used by the professional pilots. We also can use role-playing exercises to prepare for difficult choices and improve our chances of success.

Here's how it works. Sit down with parents, friends, or Church leaders. Let them choose one of the scenarios listed below, or perhaps create a scenario of their own, and present it to you. Put yourself in the situation and role-play how you would handle it. What do you do? What choice do you make? Can you apply the Agency Checklist? Discuss what you might say, how you might behave, what action you might need to take in order to choose the right. When you are done role-playing, discuss the lessons learned and commit to applying them to real-life situations in the future. Have fun with them. Learn from them. Most

The Agency Checklist

In all situations—

✓ Maintain Agency Control

- At all times—keep your agency

✓ Analyze the Choice

- How will this decision affect my life?

- What decision will maintain my values?

- Have I made this decision already?

✓ Exercise Your Agency Appropriately

- Choose the right!

✓ Get to Safety as Soon as Conditions Permit

- Put yourself in a "safe" environment

- Talk about your decision with a parent/mentor/leader

important, use these scenarios to increase your chances of agency success.

Are you ready? Feel free to reference the checklist above to help you succeed. *Exercise your agency*!

Scenario 1: The Test

You are taking a test in history class, and it's much harder than you expected. While you are struggling to answer the difficult questions, the teacher gets called out into the hallway to speak with the principal. When he steps out of the room, many of the students around you quickly consult their notes or their textbooks to cheat on the test. You know the teacher grades on a curve, and you are struggling to get a B in the class. Your notes, with the answers to several questions, are in your backpack at your feet. What do you do?

Scenario 2: Drugs at a Party

You go to a party with some friends. The music is loud, and everyone is having a good time. You take a seat on the couch next to a girl you know and strike up a conversation. After a few minutes, she pulls out a bag of marijuana joints and says with a laugh, "I got a prescription for this stuff. Does anyone want to try it?" She takes one and offers you the bag and a lighter. How will you react?

Scenario 3: Game or Tithing?

You have been saving your money to buy a new video game about to be released. All your friends are buying the game and want to play head-to-head with you as soon as it is released. The day it goes on sale you have just enough to buy it, but then you remember that you still need to pay tithing. If you set aside money for tithing, you won't have enough for the game. Will you buy the game or pay tithing?

Scenario 4: Prevalent Pornography

You get a group message on your phone from a buddy in your gym class. When you open the message, you see multiple pornographic images. How will you handle this situation?

Scenario 5: Social Media Bullying

You check your social media account before school and notice that it has exploded with comments about a shy girl in your math class. The comments are hateful and ridiculing. When you get to math class, you don't see her. Everyone in the class is talking about the comments and mocking her. What will you do?

Scenario 6: Time Card

You arrive at work a few minutes early. One of your coworkers sends you a text: "I'm running late. Punch my time card for me so I don't get docked for being late." Nobody is around, and your boss is on vacation. Will you punch your friend's time card for her?

Scenario 7: Inspection

You are in charge of a medical facility that is being audited by government regulators. One of the auditors approaches you demanding documentation that you followed proper protocol with a specific patient. When you go to retrieve the paperwork, it is missing. You know that you followed protocol, and if you fill out a new form and backdate it, no one will ever know. Will you backdate the form or accept responsibility for the mistake?

Scenario 8: Party Time

A cute, popular girl from English class invites you to an exclusive party. You are thrilled at the prospect.

You check the calendar and realize the party is on Sunday, during sacrament meeting. Will you go to the party or sacrament meeting?

Scenario 9: Sunset

The hot guy from geography class asks you on a date. All the other girls are jealous. He picks you up in his new pickup truck and drives you to a secluded spot and backs the truck up to a cliff with a spectacular view of the sunset. He removes the bed cover on the truck to reveal a mattress with blankets. He slips off his shirt and invites you to cuddle with him in the back of the truck as the sun goes down. What do you do?

How did you do? Did you maintain agency control? Did you analyze the situation correctly? Did you always choose the right? Did you get to a safe place and discuss the lessons learned? No matter what you chose, did you learn from the role-playing exercise? Did these scenarios help you prepare to use your agency in a stressful situation?

The list of scenarios is by no means exhaustive or complete. Life will constantly throw curveballs at you and keep you guessing, but with the help of parents, teachers, and leaders that have more experience, you can practice and prepare to use your agency in a wide variety of situations. Ask parents and leaders to share their stories of difficult decisions and problematic choices. Come up with a few scenarios of your own. If you practice choosing the right *before* the choice is placed before you, it increases your ability to choose the right when you are actually faced with the choice.

Prepare to exercise your agency like a fighter pilot preparing for the ejection decision, and you will be better prepared to exercise your agency and choose a righteous path automatically. Learn to employ all the resources available to you: the scriptures, prayer, the Holy Ghost, Church leaders, and parents. Our chances of choosing the right improve dramatically when we practice choosing the right and use all the resources available to us. My prayer is that through proper preparation and practice, you will make the decision to choose the right an automatic one. Then, just like Captain Stricklin, when you are faced with a split-second decision, your training will kick in and help you choose the right.

WHAT HAPPENS IF YOU CRASH?

Even the best of pilots have bad days. Many an expert aviator has made a serious, or perhaps even fatal, mistake. Both of the Wright brothers crashed more than once. Charles Lindbergh, the first pilot to cross the Atlantic Ocean solo in an airplane, crashed and bailed out of an airplane. Captain Christopher Stricklin, a handpicked Thunderbird Pilot, made one mental error that led to his ejection and the fiery destruction of a perfectly good airplane in the middle of an airshow. In spite of the best training, the best intentions, and the best preparation, pilots make mistakes.

A few years ago, I evaluated two pilots in the B-737 simulator during their annual check ride. (A check ride is like a driving test but conducted in an advanced simulator that can simulate emergencies.) They came to the simulator well prepared for the event. They had studied diligently. They had practiced the various maneuvers and emergency situations. They were professionals in their demeanor and conduct. In spite of all that preparation and good intent, the check ride did not end well.

On one of the takeoffs, an engine failed and caught on fire. The two pilots began to handle the problem. They quickly announced their intentions to shut down the problematic engine and started to do so. Unfortunately, they rushed the decision and their actions. They hurried without confirming their action and shut down the engine that was operating normally—the only good engine they had left. Now they were only a few hundred feet above the ground with an engine that wasn't working and the good engine shut down.

At first they were shocked, but realizing their mistake they hurriedly tried to restart the engine they had unintentionally turned off. However, they were too close to the ground and the simulation ended with the aircraft crashing into the ground and killing all the simulated passengers on board. Two excellent pilots rushed and made a fatal mistake. Fortunately, it was during a simulation.

It was a painful experience for two well-prepared and professional pilots, but they learned from the experience. They successfully completed their retraining and were soon back in the cockpit flying passengers safely to their destinations. Today they are both better pilots because of the experience. Their past mistake did not define their future.

Joseph Smith was called and chosen to be a prophet of God and restore the gospel to earth. The story of his First Vision is miraculous. The truths revealed through him are astounding. The priesthood restored through him is essential to conducting God's work on the earth. The Prophet Joseph was a chosen and inspired man, but he was not perfect. He didn't always make the right choice.

In 1827, while Joseph Smith was translating the Book of Mormon, he was befriended and helped by Martin Harris, a well-to-do farmer who sometimes acted as scribe. Martin was under tremendous pressure from friends and family members to prove that Joseph Smith was a prophet and actually had the golden plates, so he pleaded with the Prophet Joseph to loan him the manuscript. Joseph went to the Lord in prayer and was instructed to not allow it. Martin Harris pressured Joseph even more, and Joseph returned to the Lord in prayer twice more with the same result. Finally, after persistent pleading, the Lord allowed Joseph to loan 116 pages of the manuscript to Martin Harris.

Unfortunately, while the 116 pages were in Martin Harris's possession, they were either stolen or lost. When he learned of this, Joseph exclaimed, "What shall I do? I have sinned—it is I who tempted the wrath of God. I should have been satisfied with the first answer which I received from the Lord" (*Our Heritage: A Brief History of The Church of Jesus Christ of Latter-day Saints*, 8). For a brief period the golden plates and the Urim and Thumim were taken from Joseph. As you can imagine, it was dark time for the Prophet Joseph. His gift was taken. The revelations from heaven ceased for a period. He was sorely chastened for his error.

After a period of repentance, Joseph was forgiven and continued the work. The Lord instructed him, "Nevertheless, it is now restored unto you again; therefore see that you are faithful and continue on unto the finishing of the remainder of the work of translation as you have begun" (D&C 10:3). He also advised him, "Pray always, that you may come off conqueror; yea, that you may conquer Satan, and that you may escape the hands of the servants of Satan that do uphold his work" (D&C10:5).

The great Prophet Joseph Smith made an error, but he did not allow that lapse in judgment stop him from completing his work. He humbled himself, repented, and continued faithfully in the Lord's work. He went on to do "more, save Jesus only, for the salvation of men in this world, than any other man that ever lived in it" (D&C 135:3). We are all blessed because of it.

If the best of pilots make mistakes, and even prophets sometimes commit error, what will we do? Are we infallible? Are we safe from errors in judgment or even outright disobedience? No. We will all make mistakes. We will all sin. "If we say that we have no sin, we deceive ourselves, and the truth is not in us" (1 John 1:8). In pilot terms, we will all crash.

What happens when we crash?

The simulator used for training pilots is very realistic and acts and feels like the airplane, except when it comes to crashing. With the touch of a button it can simulate various flight conditions, weather phenomena, and aircraft malfunctions. When a pilot makes mistakes or mishandles an emergency situation, the simulator will re-create a crash just like in the airplane, except that no one will get hurt. This allows instructors to put pilots into very difficult situations without actually risking anyone's life. It also allows for pilots to learn from their mistakes in a realistic environment without risking their own lives.

The computer panel for controlling the simulator has a very important button—the crash override button. That button will allow the pilot to keep flying even if the conditions would have produced a crash. With the crash override button, we can simply reset the simulation and try again without any damage or injury.

Life is like a giant simulation. We have come here to earth to gain a body and be tested. Heavenly Father knew we would all sin during this process. So He provided us a way to overcome sin through the Atonement of Christ. It is a perfect plan that allows us the moral agency to choose for ourselves (sometimes incorrectly) and yet not suffer eternally when we choose disobedience. Like the two pilots that rushed and crashed in the simulator, we can also be retrained and continue our lives through the power of the Atonement.

The retraining process for life is called repentance. Repentance allows us to recover from our mistakes and disobedience. It allows us to learn from our errors and continue forward with our lives. It allows us to wipe away any damage caused by sin. Repentance will return us to our previous state without permanent injury or damage. When we repent, we reset our lives so we can try again, except now we will be wiser.

Additionally, we can use the "debrief" as a powerful tool to improve our own agency performance. When we "crash" and make a poor choice, a thorough debrief with a leader, mentor, or friend can help us capture the lessons learned from the experience. Just like a thorough investigation after an aircraft accident, we need to investigate our spiritual crash and learn from the experience so we don't repeat it.

Perhaps, we got into a fight with a sibling and lost our temper. After our temper has cooled and our thinking has returned to reasonable and rational, we can take some time to reconstruct the event and determine why we lost our temper. What triggered our anger? When was the exact moment when we felt ourselves lose control? With that moment clear in our mind, we can build a space for agency. We can look back through the lens of time and see other options we could have chosen. During this debrief, we can then practice how we will choose differently in the future. We need not be slaves to our past habits, and the "debrief" is a powerful tool for breaking the bad habits of our past and replacing them with good habits.

Think of life as a giant simulation. We experience a series of challenging scenarios and difficult situations that teach and test us. When we make mistakes or fail in one situation, we cannot think that our entire life is lost and give up. We can be retrained and try again because of the Atonement. Life is a series of tests and retests, not one final exam. Keep trying!

A woman, caught in the very act of adultery, was brought to Jesus by the Scribes and Pharisees. The law of Moses demanded that she be stoned for her disobedience. In an attempt to catch Jesus in a dogmatic trap, they explained the situation and asked, "What sayest thou?" (John 8:5). He assessed the situation and instead of answering at first, stooped down and wrote in the dirt with his finger. Growing impatient, his detractors pressed him for an answer.

Jesus arose from the ground and said, "He that is without sin among you, let him first cast a stone at her" (John 8:5). Then he stooped back down and continued to write in the dirt with his finger. (We can only speculate what he was writing, but it must have been powerful.) After a few minutes, the accusers, pricked with their own shame, dispersed and left the woman with Jesus.

Jesus arose and asked, "Woman, where are those thine accusers? hath no man condemned thee? She said, No man, Lord. And Jesus said unto her, Neither do I condemn thee: go, and sin no more" (John 8:10–11). What a beautiful example of the Savior's grace and power to save from sin!

The law condemned her to a punishment, but through the grace and mercy of the Atonement of Christ, He bore that punishment for her. He can do the same for us. He can send our accusers away. He can answer the demands of justice and show us mercy. He can give us the opportunity to "go and sin no more" (John 8:11). The Atonement enables us to reset our lives and try again. Through the grace, mercy, and saving power of the Atonement of Christ, "all mankind may be saved by obedience to the laws and ordinances of the Gospel" (Third Article of Faith).

Just like the simulator that allows us to reset and try again, the Atonement is the ultimate crash override button for life. The Atonement allows us to recover from our mistakes, our misdeeds, and even our intentional sins. Each time we exercise faith in the Atonement and repent, it's like we "reset" the simulation of our life and try again to get it right. Christ has already paid the price for our crashes. His Atonement can override any sin we have committed if we repent.

Crash trucks are standing by. All airports are equipped with emergency response equipment and personnel trained to react quickly in case of an aircraft accident or crash. The fire trucks are designed especially for dealing with fuel fires or extracting people from a damaged aircraft fuselage. The emergency personnel are specifically trained to find the crash site in bad weather and administer aid to passengers in shock as they egress from a damaged airplane. They have the equipment and the training to help in the moment of crisis.

When trouble arises and a pilot realizes that a problem with an aircraft may lead to dangerous landing or likely crash, he or she makes a radio call and declares an emergency. Declaring an emergency is a cry for help. Declaring an emergency puts emergency personnel on alert and they rush to their trucks and wait by the runway for the emergency aircraft to land. All pilots know that all they have to do is declare an emergency, and all those emergency resources will be standing by.

Likewise, spiritual crash trucks are also standing by. Church leaders are equipped with priesthood keys and special spiritual equipment to help pull you from the wreckage of a crash. Your parents and teachers are trained in the gospel and can rescue you from a spiritually damaging situation or choice. Everyone from the prophet to your parents stands ready to help you when you crash. All you have to do is declare a spiritual emergency by reaching out to them in interviews, conversations, or through study. When you crash, spiritual crash trucks are standing by to assist with love.

Even the best pilots make mistakes. Even prophets are mortal and commit error. We are not infallible. We will crash. But when we do, the event doesn't have to be final. Christ did not sin, and because of His infinite Atonement, we need not suffer the effects of a spiritual crash forever. Declare a spiritual emergency. Repent. Debrief. Try again. His grace is sufficient.

CONCLUSION

In the high-speed world of aviation, milliseconds can be the difference between life and death. How is it possible for pilots to make the correct life-or-death decision in milliseconds? They don't wait until they are faced with the difficult decision to decide what to do. Successful pilots prepare ahead of time to deal with dangerous situations through study, training, and practice. If we wish to use our agency effectively and make spiritual life-or-death decisions in milliseconds, we must do the same. We must prepare and train to choose the right.

When Christ was ready to begin his full-time ministry, He spent some time alone in the wilderness "to be with God" (Joseph Smith Translation, Matthew 4:1). He understood this principle of preparation. He knew that He would face great trials and challenges, and He set aside time to prepare for them. During this time of preparation, the devil came and tempted Him. Using scriptural references to rebuke the tempter, Christ successfully avoided temptation and came off conqueror. We should do likewise.

Think about the type of person you want to be *now*. The choices we make in life will ultimately define who we are. Don't leave the important choices up to chance. Prepare *now* to make the critical choices that will determine your character. Who will you decide to be?

Rehearse *now* how you will handle difficult choices. Life can surprise us with some unexpected challenges. We can't always predict what tomorrow will bring, but we can prepare by rehearsing the difficult choices we might face. We don't need to wait for life to surprise us. Rehearsing through role-playing can help us prepare *now* for life's difficult choices.

Decide *now* to choose the right. Like President Spencer W. Kimball advised, "You only need to decide some things *once!*" ("President Kimball Speaks Out on Planning Your Life"). Spend some time pondering the common moral decisions of life. Learn to listen to and recognize the promptings of the Holy Ghost. Decide to choose the right through preparation and study, and then follow through with that decision every time you are faced with the choice. President Thomas S. Monson said, "May we ever choose the harder right instead of the easier wrong" ("Choices").

Prepare *now* to choose the right.

Agency is one of God's greatest gifts. It is essential to His plan. Like trained pilots, we can follow a checklist for using our agency. The Agency Checklist can help keep us from overlooking or forgetting important steps to exercising our moral agency effectively. Great gifts must be used with wisdom and care.

Remember that even the best of pilots make mistakes. Crash trucks are standing by. The power of the Atonement is real. Christ is our ultimate instructor, evaluator, and rescuer. He stands ready with outstretched arms to rescue us from the fiery crashes and ejections of life. He alone offers us the grace sufficient to save us from certain spiritual death when we crash. The Atonement is the ultimate crash override button.

The fighter pilot has three choices in any life-threatening situation—fly, eject, or die. He can continue to fly the airplane, provided that it will still fly, and eventually land it. He can eject and hope that the ejection and parachute all work as advertised. He can crash with the airplane and most likely die. Even though it seems like the ejection decision is made in milliseconds, preparation for the ejection decision has taken hours, even days. Training, preparation, and practice have prepared the fighter pilot to make a split-second, life-or-death decision.

Like the fighter pilot, we are faced with spiritual life-and-death decisions with only milliseconds to decide. Learning to properly exercise our agency takes preparation. It takes training. It takes practice. Like the professional pilot, we can make the decision to choose the right long before we are faced with the decision. Then, when the choice is placed before us, we will choose the right—automatically.

WORKS CITED

Amidon, SSGT Jamie, National Archives Catalog.
"Photograph 6648672." Accessed Aug. 8, 2016.
https://catalog.archives.gov/id/6648672.

"Choose the Right," *Hymns*, no. 239.

Christofferson, D. Todd, "Moral Agency," *Speeches.byu.
edu*. Brigham Young University, 16 Aug. 2007.
Accessed Jan. 25, 2016. http://speeches.byu.
edu/?act=viewitem&id=1515.

Church of Jesus Christ of Latter-day Saints, The. *Our
Heritage: A Brief History of The Church of Jesus
Christ of Latter-day Saints* (Salt Lake City, UT:
Church of Jesus Christ of Latter-day Saints,
1996).

Davis, SSGT Bennie J., "National Archives Catalog," *National Archives Catalog*. Department of Defense, 30 Jan. 2004. Accessed Aug. 8, 2016. https://catalog.archives.gov/id/6628813.

Eyring, Henry B., "The Holy Ghost as Your Companion," *Ensign*, November 2015.

Freeman, Gregory A., "22 Seconds," *Reader's Digest*, 1 Feb. 2005. 161–66.

Fuqua, SSGT Mitch, *National Archives Catalog*, "Photograph 6513816." Accessed Aug. 8, 2016. https://catalog.archives.gov/id/6513816.

Hales, Robert D., "The Aaronic Priesthood: Return with Honor," *Ensign*, May, 1990.

Kimball, Spencer W., "President Kimball Speaks Out on Planning Your Life," *New Era*, Sept. 1981.

Ludlow, Daniel H., "Moral Free Agency," *BYU Speeches*, Brigham Young University, 11 Aug. 2014. Accessed Aug. 9, 2016. https://speeches.byu.edu/talks/daniel-h-ludlow_moral-free-agency/.

McKay, David O., "The Improvement Era," Editorial. *Improvement Era* 1 Feb. 1962: 16–17. *The Improvement Era*. 18 July 2012. Accessed

Jan. 25, 2016. https://archive.org/stream/
improvementera6502unse#page/n15/
mode/2up.

Monson, Thomas S., "Choices," *Ensign,* May 2016.

Monson, Thomas S., "The Holy Temple—a Beacon to
the World," *Ensign,* May 2011.

National Aviation Hall of Fame.,"Link, Edwin Albert
- National Aviation Hall of Fame," *National
Aviation Hall of Fame*, Accessed 20 Jan. 2016.
http://www.nationalaviation.org/link-edwin/.

National Archives Catalog. "Photograph No.
6513816." https://catalog.archives.gov/
id/6513816.

National Archives Catalog. "Photograph No.
6648672." https://catalog.archives.gov/
id/6648672.

National Transportation Safety Board, "NTSB
Releases Final Report on Investigation of
Crash of Aircraft Piloted by John F. Ken-
nedy Jr." Accessed Jul. 29, 2016. http://www.
ntsb.gov/news/press-releases/Pages/NTSB_
NTSB_releases_final_report_on_investi-
gation_of_crash_of_aircraft_piloted_by_
John_F._Kennedy_Jr.aspx.

National Transportation Safety Board, "Accident Reports." Accessed Feb. 10, 2016. http://www. ntsb.gov/investigations/AccidentReports/ Reports/AAR0201.pdf.

National Transportation Safety Board, "Accident Reports." Accessed Feb. 10, 2016. http://www. ntsb.gov/investigations/AccidentReports/ Reports/AAR1401.pdf.

National Transportation Safety Board, "Accident Reports." Accessed Feb. 8, 2016. http://www. ntsb.gov/investigations/AccidentReports/ Reports/AAR7314.pdf.

Federal Aviation Administration, "Human Factors in Aviation Maintenance." Accessed Feb. 8, 2016. http://www.faa.gov/about/initiatives/mainte- nance_hf/library/documents/media/human_fac- tors_maintenance/united_airlines_flight_232. mcdonnell_douglas_dc-10-10.sioux_gateway_ airport.sioux_city.Iowa.july_19.1989.pdf.

National Transportation Safety Board, "Accident Reports." http://www.ntsb.gov/investigations/ AccidentReports/Reports/AAR1401.pdf.

PlaneCrashInfo.com. Accessed Feb. 15, 2016. http:// www.planecrashinfo.com/cause.htm.

Ranter, Harro, "Despite High Profile Accidents, 2014 Was the Safest Year Ever According to ASN Data," *ASN News*. Aviation Safety Network, 01 Jan. 2015. Web. 10 Feb. 2016. http://news. aviation-safety.net/2015/01/01/despite-high-profile-accidents-2014-was-the-safest-year-ever-according-to-asn-data/.

Steinbeck, John, *East of Eden* (New York: Penguin, 2002), 301.

United States Air Force. *T.O. 1A-10A-1 Flight Manual A-10A Aircraft*. USAF, 1988. 282. Print.

Wikipedia contributors, "List of countries and dependencies by number of police officers," Wikipedia, The Free Encyclopedia. Accessed Jan. 20, 2016. https://en.wikipedia. org/w/index.php?title=List_of_countries_ and_dependencies_by_number_of_police_ officers&oldid=733527808.

Wikipedia contributors, "Split S," Wikipedia, The Free Encyclopedia. Accessed Aug. 29, 2016. https://en.wikipedia.org/w/index.php?title=Sp lit_S&oldid=700191140.

Acknowledgments

Over fifteen years ago my brother-in-law Jared Hancock invited me to speak to the young men and women in his ward. He asked me to discuss my flying experiences and relate them to the gospel. Almost immediately the premise this book is built on came to mind. I put a presentation together and kept from boring the youthful audience to tears. From time to time I would be invited to speak at youth firesides or conferences, and I always enjoyed delivering the message of preparation and decision-making. Each time I added more material. Each time I honed the message. Each time I enjoyed my interaction with the wonderful young men and women of our Church.

A few years ago, my wife, Britt, urged me to turn the presentation into book form. She felt the concept would fly, but I was uncertain. I made excuses for months, but in the end she persisted. This book would not have been written except for the urging of my supportive and persistent wife.

As is my usual pattern, I turned to experts for sound advice with this project. First, I bounced it off my writing group—Randy Lindsay, Ryan Hancock, Adrienne Quintana, Jannette Rallison, Aaron Blaylock, and Laura Walker. Each of them encouraged me. Each of them gave me sound critical advice for turning a presentation into book form. Each of them helped me believe in my abilities. I am a better man and a better writer because of them. If you ever want to hear a bunch of writers having fun, just go to www.readysetwritepodcast.com.

Next, I turned to friends with both a sound spiritual foundation and a keen eye for good content. My sister-in-law Jennifer Hancock has always been willing to read my manuscripts and wade through the clunky sentences and incoherent paragraphs while picking out the gems and polishing them for me. My friend and coworker, Marcus North (fighter pilot extraordinaire), understands and lives the concepts presented in this book, and helped me focus more on the Atonement. My friend Wade Whiting helped me see the profound impact a good mentor can have on someone struggling after a crash. Heidi Tucker, an excellent writer and presenter, showed me through her example that stories can change lives for the better. Ty Ruddell, my friend and chiropractor for almost fifteen years, invited me to speak to the youth of his stake and encouraged me to expand the message of this book. Todd Nuttall filled me with his enthusiasm for the topic. Adam Zamorra allowed me to use a scenario from his life and share the lessons he learned.

All of my children, Rian, Cody, Sarah, Kati, Carson, and Rylee, have put up with my writing habit, my boring lectures, and a few catastrophic spiritual crashes of my own. My life would be incomplete without the love of my children.

I offer special thanks to Christopher Stricklin. As I was preparing to write this book, we corresponded. He was gracious and courageous. Aviators can be jealous, cynical, and quick to highlight the errors of fellow aviators. His ejection decision was flawless. I am neither jealous nor cynical of his performance. I offer no criticism of his abilities as an aviator. His skillful application of training in an impossible situation saved lives. I salute him.

As always, I am sure I have forgotten people who have enriched my life, expanded my vision, or encouraged me directly or indirectly to write this book. Even though writing a book can be a lonely process, I cannot do it without the help of thousands.

ABOUT THE AUTHOR

B rock Booher grew up on a farm in Kentucky, the fourth of ten children. One day while he was out working the fields in the hot summer sun, a low-flying military jet came screaming overhead, barely missing the trees, and disappeared like a shooting star. Right then he decided that flying looked like more fun than farming. He left the farm in pursuit of his dream, graduated from Brigham Young University, and headed off to pilot training as a new 2nd Lieutenant in the United States Air Force. When he was selected to fly the A-10, he became the low-flying pilot buzzing young farm boys in the fields of Europe and Northern Iraq. He went on to serve as an Instructor Pilot and Section Chief of Academics in the T-37. Fluent in Spanish, he also served in the United States Embassy in Lima,

Peru, helping with counternarcotic operations. He transitioned to commercial airline flying in the Boeing 737 and has over fifteen thousand hours of flying time. As a Certified Ground Instructor, Check Airman, and Standards Check Airman, he has instructed and evaluated hundreds of pilots in the classroom, the simulator, and the aircraft.

In addition to his pursuits as a pilot, he has taught courses on time management, risk management, leadership, and goal setting. He has volunteered in the classroom as an Adopt-A-Pilot for over ten years teaching fifth graders about science, math, and careers. He enjoys stretching his creativity through writing, and his works have been published in magazines, nonfiction books, short stories, and novels.

He has been married to his wife, Britt, for almost thirty years, and she has molded him into a better man. They have six wonderfully independent children and one adorable grandson. In spite of all the time he spends in airplanes, he still loves to travel, especially when it involves a bit of adventure or service.

You can follow him at www.brockbooher.com, on Facebook (AuthorBrockBooher) and on Twitter (@BrockBooher).